Culture Savvy

Culture Savvy

Working and Collaborating Across the Globe

Maureen Bridget Rabotin

ASTD
PRESS

Alexandria, Virginia

ASTD Press is an internationally renowned source of insightful and practical information on workplace learning and performance topics, including training basics, evaluation and return-on-investment, instructional systems development, e-learning, leadership, and career development.

Ordering information: Books published by ASTD Press can be purchased by visiting ASTD's website at store.astd.org or by calling 800.628.2783 or 703.683.8100.

Library of Congress Control Number: 2009939982

ISBN-10: 1-56286-736-9
ISBN-13: 978-1-56286-736-2

ASTD Press Editorial Staff:
Director: Anthony Allen
Manager, ASTD Press: Larry Fox
Project Manager, Content Acquisition: Justin Brusino
Senior Associate Editor: Tora Estep
Associate Editor: Ashley McDonald
Editorial Assistant: Stephanie Castellano
Copyeditor: Alfred Imhoff
Indexer: April Michelle Davis
Proofreader: Kristy S. Patenaude
Interior Design and Production: PerfecType, Nashville, TN
Cover Design: Ana Ilieva Foreman
Cover Art: www.gettyimages.com, imagewerks
Printed by Versa Press Inc., East Peoria, IL, www.versapress.com

Contents

Foreword

Organizations operate in an increasingly complex, multicultural, and global context. Cultural differences are often a source of misunderstanding, frustration, and even derailment (particularly in cross-border mergers and acquisitions). However, when leveraged, cultural diversity becomes a source of creativity and an opportunity to go beyond current limitations.

With curiosity, openness, and eagerness to learn from other cultures, new choices and fresh perspectives become available to us. In this new book, *Culture Savvy: Working and Collaborating Across the Globe,* Maureen Bridget Rabotin looks at how social media and globalization can bring forth opportunities while understanding the advances in neuroscience that remind us that we are humans seeking collaboration and compassion. *Culture Savvy* contributes to promoting unity in place of fragmentation. This is much needed in today's world.

—Philippe Rosinski, executive coach, author, professor, and principal of Rosinski and Company

In his book *Coaching Across Cultures,* Rosinski shows how to reach sustainable and meaningful success and how to achieve unity in diversity by systematically integrating the crucial cultural dimension into coaching. In his most recent book, *Global Coaching,* he presents the Cultural Orientations Framework assessment and shows how a dynamic and inclusive cultural approach can be used in practice with individuals, teams, and organizations. I had the pleasure of meeting Philippe Rosinski at the ICF

European conference in Brussels, Belgium, in 2006. His work and vision were an inspiration for this book—*Culture Savvy: Working and Collaborating Across the Globe.*

—Maureen Bridget Rabotin, global executive coach
and founder of Effective Global Leadership

Acknowledgments

How do I thank so many people across the globe who have inspired me, and edged me on, encouraging me to be the lifelong learner I am today? Gratitude for wanting to know more—about myself and about others goes to

- Jean-Jacques, Jenny, and Chris, for respecting my need to have the time and space to write this book, as well as my extended family for their encouragement.

- Anne, Peter, Angela, and David, for their friendship and coaching support. Paul, Brian, and Jan for their research on values and principles. Kevin and Bjorn for their tools. And all my colleagues around the world, in particular Andrea, who read, commented, agreed, and disagreed with what I wanted to write. Those exchanges were what I call high-quality conversations.

- The survey respondents—too many to name here—who all sent sincere wishes of good luck while giving me their permission to publish, to share their dream of breaking down barriers and building bridges of understanding. These virtual relationships have been my inspiration.

- And, of course, to my clients across the globe—from luxury goods, to pharmaceuticals, to nongovernmental organizations. Some wanting a simple list of what to do and what not to do, all wanting better relationships where respect, recognition, and rewards make for a better workplace.

I extend my sincere appreciation to each and all of you, and acknowledge that without your support, I would not have found the courage to embark on such a learning curve. Sincere thanks go to Justin at ASTD Press, who recognized my passion in an article I wrote, and then gave me the opportunity to work with Alfred, who has been my guiding light during these last months. I don't think this book would have ever materialized if our relationship had not been as rewarding as it was. Thank you all, and apologies to those I may have overlooked in this list. Any mistakes or omissions are not with willfulness or intent.

Introduction:
The Challenge and
Opportunity of
Cross-Cultural Cooperation

Get them to think out of the box. There's something missing.
In meetings, they wait to be called on. They defer to others.
What makes "them" so different?

—A corporate sponsor, while signing a coaching contract

As globalization accelerates like a whirlwind around us, the need to step back, refocus, and realign our objectives has never been more important. If our desired outcome is to work more effectively and collaborate more efficiently with colleagues, managers, and partners from different cultures, whether in our own workplace or around the world, we must shift our perspective from a local to a more global worldview. The speed with which we are able to adapt to foreign behaviors and unfamiliar environments will be the make-or-break dimension of future business deals and the foundation for ruptured or resonant relationships.

As companies painstakingly enter into and try to succeed in the globalization process, the question of culture—meaning the portrayal of our everyday behaviors, derived from the combination of our beliefs, assumptions, and values, along with implicit (mis)understandings—is part of the formula. Cross-cultural understanding, which was once a desirable attribute for those employees who travel, has now become an absolute necessity for everyone who could receive a tweet from someone in Delhi

1

or who needs to work on a project via Skype with someone in Reykjavik. In our globalized—and globally dispersed—workplaces, culture persists, but cross-cultural cooperation lingers behind as a challenge to overcome and not yet the rewarding opportunity it ought to be.

Budget cuts and overbooked agendas have companies putting e-learning and cross-cultural crash courses high on their to-do lists with hopes that these programs will diminish the challenges inherent in cultural differences. The unfortunate outcome? In trying to be "politically correct," we avoid any real discussion with and about our colleagues from other cultures.

Becoming Culture Savvy

What can you do differently to get off the high-speed technological raceway and put a human face on your colleagues around the world—and those from different cultures in your own workplace? This is the question I have asked myself and many participants in the cross-cultural training events I have been doing since 1996. What I hope to achieve with this book is to help you answer this question, to enable you to function effectively in the cross-cultural context of the globalized workplace. Of course, there is certainly more than one answer to this question, but simply pondering how to answer it can help you begin to make changes in your behavior, thus engendering a climate of cross-cultural receptivity.

As a starter, I would like to suggest that you empty your mind of the stereotypes and cultural biases we all carry around with us. The next time an idea that involves categorizing people comes to mind—all Americans are like that, or the Chinese always react that way—stop yourself. Remind yourself that such generalizations lead to preconceived ideas. From now on, adapt your worldview by shifting your mindset. Instead of putting people and cultures in pretty little boxes according to national origins, let's make culture part of the conversation, not the shadow that looms behind failed communication, floundering projects, or unintended slights.

Becoming *culture savvy* means gaining the ability to perceive culture not as a list of differences but as the added value that expands our worldviews and cultural perspectives. Leaving behind the dualistic dimensions and linear, nationalistic approach to cultural orientations, the chapters that follow explore the cultural complexity of individuals and organizations. You'll see that culture is just one of the systems that helps make human beings unique. By accepting that every person carries with him or her a valuable and distinct culture, you will stop asking how others leverage cultural differences and instead begin to ask how each of us brings forth our own culture as the added value of who we are and what we bring to the table.

As you become culture savvy, the goal is for you to become aware of your own culture and those of others, so that cultural differences cease to be impediments and instead become easy, everyday parts of your conversations, teams, and organizations. Then you can begin to laugh at yourself, and with your colleagues around the world. In this book, you'll see that humor is essential to building trusting relationships. At many training sessions, my parting words are "Take your business seriously, not yourselves."

It's time to let go of the us-versus-them perspective reflected in the words of the corporate sponsor in the epigraph at the beginning of this introduction. The world is technologically flatter, faster, and far more interdependent than we could have imagined even 10 years ago. Respecting and recognizing our own and others' inner cultural values—those differences and expectations we've all created through our personal and professional experiences—will build the foundation for a more creative environment.

Suppressing or refusing to acknowledge cultural differences creates dissonance and unresolved conflict. And, although many well-intentioned companies put employees through a "Culture 101" training course as a first step toward developing cultural awareness, the content and format of these classes often thwart attempts to achieve a realistic perspective. Handouts with lists of "what to do" and "what not to do" in certain countries further reinforce negative stereotypes and increase anxiety about overseas collaborations. After completing such cultural crash courses, employees now "know" that the Americans are on time, the French are always late, the Japanese are emotionally neutral, the Spanish are not, and, of course, the Germans are rigorous and straightforward. Instead of acting as a guide or a hand to hold as we cross cultural and linguistic barriers, these "truisms" may very well promote the development of mental models or paradigms that we then look for—and frequently find. These mini-training techniques leave the "graduates" with a false sense of confidence and a list of how to "fake it until you make it." In effect, the risk is in promoting simple solutions for understanding the complexity of national cultures, thus reinforcing stereotypes.

I have brought my years of experience as a cross-cultural training consultant and global executive coach to this book, which presents a new approach that will help you become culture savvy and prepare you to work and collaborate in any culture. The book delves into the differences between training (transferring knowledge) and coaching (transforming people). Early intercultural research that devised country profiles was funded to facilitate understanding in international arenas. But that was more than 30 years ago. Since then, the geographic boundaries that once defined people have been evolving. In 1990, the European Schengen Agreement put an end to custom controls among 25 countries in Europe; the Berlin Wall came down more than 20 years ago; and we've now had the Internet for more than 40 years.

Today, therefore, an employee from Germany sent to a factory in Dublin will most likely be managing more Polish and Indian employees than Irish people. Everywhere in the world, mergers and acquisitions and strategic partnerships bring people together through technological means. People around the globe come together at local festivities in the streets, at neighborhood block parties, and in boardrooms, with cultures mixing to celebrate Christmas, Hanukkah, the end of Ramadan, or Chinese New Year.

Our world has changed—and so must our ways of gathering data and methodologies. As part of the research for this book, I conducted a survey of 200 people using social networks from September through November 2009. In less than three weeks, 124 people responded, confirming that they no longer wanted to be considered a statistic, that the world has changed and so have people. For these respondents, the answer to the question "Where do you come from?" has more to do with the country that issued their passport than any former identity related to political boundaries or their country of origin. This alone requires us to rethink the research from the 20th century and to reframe our questions and assumptions about national identities for the future.

The Challenge: Slow Human Nature in the Midst of Ultrafast Technology

Today's globalized, interconnected, and interdependent world has challenging changes coming at us 24 hours a day, 365 days a year, and seven days a week. Yet despite these never-ending changes, human nature essentially remains the same. How can we respond to the daily onslaught of new information and myriad possible choices when we know that the human brain works at its best when it is single-minded and focused?

One useful source of insight here is neuroscience, which is now proving that multitasking is not as efficient as some have assumed (Rosen 2008). To be both efficient and effective—doing things right and doing what is right—means following the adage "practice makes perfect," which reminds us that repeated, single-minded actions embed routines into our brain's neural pathways. This gives us a clue as to how we can learn and retain knowledge while working with colleagues around the world.

Cultural environments—where behaviors are learned—lay the foundation for perceptions of right and wrong. Whatever our age, our brains automatically reject the instability brought on by the "new and different." Without having a clear definition of why we do what we need to do, resistance is human nature's response. This may explain why some older workers balk at having to learn to use social networking media, and younger workers who tend to be early adopters become impatient with the pace of organizational change. In this situation, carefully explaining the reasons why we need to learn new technologies for some or develop patience for others can break down barriers of resistance. After all, we *can* teach old dogs new tricks (and puppies patience) because of what we now know about the brain's flexibility and durability—when there is the will to do so and there is an understanding of why we are doing it, we can learn, integrate, and adapt at any age (Just and Varma 2007).

Another aspect of this challenge is that technology is only as good as the human inputs—the old saw of "garbage in, garbage out" can apply on whole new levels. This reality is amply demonstrated by each day's news—whether the catastrophe of the Gulf of Mexico oil spill, brought on by buck passing and corner cutting in the midst of great technological sophistication, or the proliferating time-wasting aspects of various computer-assisted media. Even those human beings who are attuned to their environments and seek clarity and transparency none-theless encounter cultural differences, along with fallible human nature. Yet given this human nature, one characteristic that cuts across cultures is that bureaucracy breeds ambiguity, and hierarchy sends responsibility up, down, and sideways—avoiding accountability.

How can each of us disrupt this vicious cycle and meet the challenge of today's fast-changing, culturally diverse workplace? This book will show you how. The chapters to come explain how, as you become culture savvy by combining efficient task orientation with newly effective, culturally aware people orientation, you can have high-quality conversations and interactions with colleagues and partners around the world.

The Opportunity: Learning and Applying the Four Rs

In the midst of today's challenging, fast-changing, globalized, culturally diverse workplace, there are also great opportunities to embrace change and thus benefit from all the new cross-cultural and technological developments. To help you seize these opportunities, this book will take you on a voyage based on four principles that guide culture savvy human interaction: respect, relationships, recognition, and rewards—which I call the four Rs. Throughout the book, you'll explore the collective and individual significance of the four Rs. Here, however, it's useful to briefly delineate what I mean by each one.

Respect is understanding that communication is based on what we project and what we expect—both verbally and nonverbally. By listening attentively when others speak to us, and being authentic while adapting to circumstances and situations, we resonate a feeling that the other person has been heard. When I ask workshop participants around the globe to describe what respect looks like in their culture, they consistently answer "the feeling of being listened to." Now that we know that multitasking does not make us more efficient but instead distracts from the opportunity to have high-quality conversations—and that most everyone from any country or culture believes that the highest respect you can demonstrate to another person is to listen to him or her—what are we waiting for? It is time to put away the keyboard when someone walks into your office and focus on what that person has to say. This is how we show respect across cultures.

Relationships pertain to a combination of accountability and responsibility toward oneself and others. When we take the initiative to develop and maintain relationships, collaboration is the natural outcome. Good relationships go beyond project deadlines. When you have worked with someone and have established an equitable rapport, remembering to join them for lunch or coffee after the project has wound up is a good way of maintaining connections and staying in the loop of what is happening elsewhere in the organization. For instance, many a European has remarked on the American aptitude for asking others to be committed during deadlines but then being out of contact when nothing looms on the horizon. From one perspective, this American tendency is based on freedom and low-maintenance friendships, while in other countries, friendships and even business relationships come with bilateral obligations.

Recognition entails seeing and perceiving others' worldviews through their eyes, acknowledging their perspectives, and understanding how they feel without being drawn into their internal emotional conflicts. The simple act of acknowledging someone's participation in achieving a successful outcome will have a more lasting motivational effect than minor monetary compensation. Getting buy-in and consensus always requires the act of recognition. For example, if the contributions of those involved in a meeting are not truly recognized, the superficial, positive agreement reached during the meeting will quickly evaporate afterward, and the underlying disagreements will then emerge.

Rewards mean finding the balance between taking care of oneself—well-being—and contributing to a more meaningful purpose in life—"well-doing." These two elements, when finely tuned, can be a source of resilience in today's stressful environments. Given these basic realities, from culture to culture, opinions differ as to what designates a reward, leading to questions like these: Is it the reward itself that counts, or one's own satisfaction and the gratitude of others for having achieved something? Does the significance of a reward increase or decrease if individually received? And what if it is equally distributed among the members of a team?

As the book explores each of these four Rs, you'll visit unfamiliar landscapes and thus have the opportunity to expand your comfort zone. To comprehend and make the most of human cultural diversity, you'll first need to understand what drives each person. Accepting that each person arrives at adulthood with learned assumptions, beliefs, behaviors, and perceptions that have been formed and interpreted through the lens of his or her cultural experience is the first step toward learning how to respect, relate to, recognize, and reward him or her. This is also the starting point for your journey as the reader of this book. On this journey,

- You'll cross cultural and linguistic barriers while learning to *respect* what makes each of us unique and different.

- You'll then learn how to build *relationships* by breaking down the cultural and linguistic barriers created by perceptions and misrepresentations.

- If you can learn to understand how you are perceived by others, then you'll be able to *recognize* others for who they are and how they contribute to the bigger picture.

- Finally, you'll learn about the fourth, and often underestimated, aspect of every culture: how to truly *reward* yourself and others.

Understanding these four basic principles will enable you to better comprehend how your cultural values influence you; how, because of preconceived ideas, people tend to (mis-) judge others and why; and above all, how to adapt behaviors from other cultures without feeling the need to artificially adopt foreign mannerisms. These breakthroughs in understanding will enable you to work and collaborate around the globe with authenticity.

Thus, the basis of this book is four universal principles—respect, relationships, recognition, and rewards—that every human being seeks out and values. Over the years, our caretakers—and our educational, social, and professional environments—shape and mold these principles into particular cultural values. These values lead us to make assumptions while teaching us the acceptable behaviors that demonstrate the integrity of our principles. By being brought together in the spirit of developing cross-cultural awareness, the four R principles can become a guiding force as we venture out, stumble from time to time, and strive to succeed in this ever-changing world.

Methods

In my research for this book, as mentioned earlier, 200 people participated in a nonacademic, global survey conducted using social networks between September and November 2009. These participants—those out there living and working across generational, geographical, cultural, and linguistic barriers—revealed the feelings from the front lines.

The survey respondents, who were from 34 countries and spoke 24 languages, all enthusiastically proclaimed that cultural and linguistic barriers are coming down. Most respondents had lived in more than one country for more than six months, and, although the majority considered themselves fluent in English, only one-third were native English speakers.

Throughout this book, I'll share these survey respondents' experiences with cultural differences—from being surprised at culture clashes to being downright angry. For instance:

- You'll get a better understanding of how they felt as they tried to overcome their anxiety when it came to communicating in real-time chat rooms with their colleagues and managers.

- You'll see how habits like people's simple use of first names in some countries remains totally unheard of in others.

- You'll see how various supposedly common gestures—from shaking hands (how often?) to cheek kissing (how many times?)—will continue to cause minor setbacks in establishing rapport that we later can laugh about—together.

If you cannot learn to have conversations about cultural variations like these with your colleagues with honesty and still feel credible, then you will not be able to break down the cultural and linguistic barriers that come with working in today's highly interconnected, globalized world.

Plan of the Book

The shape of this book follows the four R principles for working effectively in a cross-cultural context—respect, relationships, recognition, and rewards. Chapter 1 introduces the four Rs in some detail, and then each R has its own successive chapter. While reading these chapters, remember that your ultimate opportunity is to integrate the four Rs and learn to adapt in this ever-changing world. Thus, by enlarging your perspective from an us/them, either/or, cause-and-effect approach, you can begin to understand that humans, with all their cultural differences and complexity, are not separate, isolated beings easily put into linear categories. In the context of this four-R approach, the universal human need to be interconnected—to belong—and our desire to find purpose in who we are and what we do can give us the courage and resilience to thrive in today's constantly changing global environment.

Chapter 1, "Culture as Context in the Globalized Workplace," explains how culture—in all its dimensions—is experienced as the primary context in the globalized workplace. Culture—those behaviors that reveal our past experiences and are defined according to our values—is the very basis of how we do things and how we perceive ourselves and others. Putting these perceptions into a global perspective allows us to step away from our innate reaction of the "right"-versus-"wrong" way of doing things. We humbly need to question our ingrained behavioral patterns and openly accept that our way may not be the only way on the high-speed technological and global highway.

Chapter 2, "Respect in the Cross-Cultural Context," explains why respect is so important in the globalized workplace and how you can engender it. Around the world, everyone wants to feel respected and to show respect toward others. This bilateral need is an underlying theme in every interaction—whether virtual or face to face. Just by becoming more attuned to our environment, we also become aware of how our nonverbal behaviors can influence others. Emotions are contagious, and positive attitudes do bring about positive results. Thus, showing respect—letting others know that you care about their opinions, input, and ideas—is often enough to get their buy-in.

Chapter 3, "Relationships: Team Building and Coaching Across Cultures," explains how gaining a better understanding of human nature and the impact of social isolation will enable you to change how you see the importance of in-groups and out-groups. Cultures often referred to as independent and other-dependent nonetheless still depend on a sense of belonging. Teams do not build themselves—they are built through respect and reliable relationships. They succeed with the help of recognition and rewards—especially those beyond monetary compensation. Learning how to ask powerful questions with the help of a coach approach can enable you to have reflective moments and begin to feel empowered, as well as encourage creativity and innovation, in turn laying the foundation for high-quality conversations and interactions.

Chapter 4, "Recognition Across Cultures," explains how recognition is important for engagement and empowerment. Finding the right amount of recognition—distributing it fairly and equitably, but above all consistently—will determine its credibility. Occasional favoritism, subjective adulation, and inconsistent compensation lead to ambiguity and a lack of trust. Dealing with these requires adhering to a performance management system based on objective and transparent performance indicators, values, and behaviors. Effective recognition unleashes innate talents within all of us. In this vein, you'll learn about the recognition initiatives you can take to release these talents within colleagues and peers around the globe. No matter the culture, everyone values being recognized for who they are and what they contribute.

Chapter 5, "Rewards Across Cultures," explains how personal and professional engagement is contingent on being appropriately rewarded. Status is reinforced in a healthy way when rewards are well calculated. But around the globe, cultural variations lead to different ways of offering rewards. For instance, on the most basic level, in some countries "thank you" is overused but in others is hardly ever used. This chapter explores differences like these, and also the reality that although rewards may not always be monetary, they are meant to motivate and engage.

Chapter 6, "Skills for Collaborating Across Cultures," distills the lessons of chapters 1 through 5. Thus, the chapter constitutes a succinct supplement and tool kit—a handy summing up to enable you to put into practice the various insights and techniques offered throughout the book for collaborating effectively across cultures. It also contains a few additional tools for engaging employees effectively to pursue true cross-cultural cooperation.

Finally, chapter 7, "The Four-R Action Plan for Working Effectively Around the Globe," brings together, in the framework of the four Rs, the enriching discoveries gleaned from working in a globalized workplace. For instance, you'll review how respectfully learning to authentically adapt will enable you to remain true to yourself while functioning effectively in culturally diverse environments. Most important, however, this chapter assists you in developing an integrated behavioral action plan for both personal and professional action based on the four Rs.

Last but not least, in an appendix, I share success stories of people who are working and collaborating around the globe.

Culture as Context in the Globalized Workplace

Culture hides much more than it reveals, and strangely enough what it hides, it hides most effectively from its own participants.

—Edward T. Hall

Globalization doesn't mean that culture will go away. Culture is and always will be one of the facets of who we are, how we present ourselves, and how we perceive others—our worldview. Globalization contributes to a more extensive meaning of what culture is and how it influences our everyday transactions—around the world or across company hallways. What makes culture more prevalent today than ever before is the proliferation of cross-cultural contacts. Just pick up the phone and you are talking with a team member you've never met; hop on an overnight flight, and you're sitting in his or her office for early morning tea working on issues that pertain to projects and people thousands of miles away.

In addition to virtual teleconferences and geodispersed project teams, you need only to look across today's typically globalized workplace to find that our various cultures come into play more and more often—sometimes subtly, sometimes abruptly, and on occasion with a culture clash. As you work with colleagues from around the globe, the natural reaction is to first notice what is different or difficult. Focusing only on differences will disintegrate a team, and looking only for similarities will promote groupthink. This book is an invitation to stop looking at differences that divide us, and to instead focus our attention on ways to understand and appreciate each other's cultural distinctiveness. A list of what to do when working with Japanese or Chinese people, or any European, would be incomplete without the human element, much like a recipe without any ingredients. Each person's genetic makeup and personal and professional experiences, along with all their desires and disappointments, bring together the full array of qualities that blend together to make up the person seated beside you or on the telephone on the other side of the planet.

What good is a static list, when you know that change itself is the only constant in life? In the world today, due to globalizing forces along with the usual historical forces, you need to look at change and people not as something you can fix to meet your standards but as something you want to learn to understand—in relation to both yourself and others. To look at change positively requires not aiming for a destination but accepting constant transformation. This is reality, and you need to change how you perceive not stability but your ability to live and work in a gyroscopic world where you're constantly recalibrating yourself, your perspective, your life. To do so, "we must learn to move beyond the mere coping with cultural differences to creating more synergy and embracing the wellspring of diversity" (Harris and Moran 1996).

Given these realities, this chapter seeks to delineate how culture forms the context for globalized workplaces. First, we look at some interesting data from the survey used as a basis for this book, which showed that more than one-third of the respondents had lived in two or three different countries by the age of 21. This shows us the rise in the multicultural person—people who have lived in more than one country and that of third-culture kids (children born in foreign countries that are not native to either of their parents).

Globalization is here to stay. So how can you prepare yourself and go beyond the primal fear factor that when left misunderstood develops into mistrust? You'll find answers to this question in this chapter. You'll learn that being more global does not require us to fly to exotic places to feel like a foreigner. Social networking media can connect you to new friends and colleagues around the globe, breaking down some of these cultural and linguistic barriers. More collaboration and more collaborative co-workers are some of the positive elements that social networks are bringing to the globalized workforce. Let's take the foreignness out of what is different and replace it with piqued curiosity, knowing that the only risk we run is to learn something new.

When you reach the end of the chapter, you'll have encountered concrete, everyday examples of how to adapt to our flatter and faster world with more ease and less stress. A little understanding of how the human brain functions explains people's primary reactions when faced with what is unfamiliar. Knowing that this is normal and that your ultimate outcome is that of success and happiness, you can begin to let go of the negative and embrace the positive aspects of change and globalization. Of course, this takes time—a precious gift of which we complain that we never have enough.

Fascinating—and Pointed—Findings: The Survey Results

The survey described in the introduction yielded findings that were indicative of the increasing exposure to global social networking media. Despite this real-time interaction with others from around the globe, the persistence of culture plays a critical role in today's globalized workplace. Cross-cultural incidents, not to mention culture clashes, still remain a challenge, generating both frustration and misunderstandings where collaborative efforts require transparency and clarity.

As mentioned earlier, these feelings were revealed from the front lines—from people living and working across generational, geographical, cultural, and linguistic barriers—by 200 participants in a nonacademic global survey conducted via social networks in September and November 2009. Respondents from 34 countries speaking 24 languages all enthusiastically proclaimed that cultural and linguistic barriers were coming down. Yet, when asked if they had recently experienced their cultural values being transgressed, 93 percent answered yes.

The survey results show that culture persists in so many often-confusing as well as delightful ways in our globalized and globally dispersed workplaces. When asked about which national culture influenced them the most, many survey respondents echoed the reply of Jorg Borgwardt: "I call the world my home." Jorg has lived in more than seven countries for more than two years at a time and has worked on all continents, and as a result he is multilingual and multicultural. (His specific qualifications include brand positioning, adapting global strategies to local needs, and negotiating remuneration systems that reward intangible contributions of agencies in a fair and sustainable manner. Today, he works as a management consultant specializing in local and regional agencies and networks.)

This is illustrative of the increasing integration of our world and the process of globalization. People are no longer focused on differences and no longer want to be put into categories. For example, consider an individual with a mother from Russia and a father from Cuba who was raised in France, educated at the International American School, and cared for by a British nanny. Which national country profile would best describe this person? The same mix of cultures and education can be found in most countries today. The first step in integrating culture into our systemic beings is to accept it as part of an intricate reality that brings value to the complexity of every person. This is not about nations or politics, but about people and attitudes.

Although the survey respondents cited opportunities and cooperation as some of the positive results of globalization, the word "globalization" still arouses fear in some. Perhaps this is because change—a process that means grappling with instability, both physically and physiologically—is an inevitable side effect of globalization. Change makes many people nervous, but it will continue to be a part of our reality. Questions that give rise to this fear often have to do with the confusion over cultural identity. Will foreign behaviors overcome my country's traditional ways of life?

One can find a clue to this fear of acculturation in the word's etymology, which includes the concept of the "alien"; the word "acculturation" originally meant "the adoption and assimilation of an alien culture" (thanks to Douglas Harper's *Online Etymological Dictionary*, www.etymonline .com). But now, years later, foreign cultures are often no longer seen as alien. Those in younger generations around the world are happy to wear jeans and T-shirts, and eat hamburgers to go instead of meals marinated for hours on end. But when it comes to challenging a cultural affinity, you only need to see which team you cheer for at an international sports competition or whose side you take in a debate. This is when the issue at hand speaks not to your national identity but to your ingrained cultural values.

However, given this cultural complexity, the meaning of culture as *context* has become quite intriguing. By context, I mean the conditions in which globalization and culture are taking on deeper significance in our daily lives. Culture is an intricate part of the challenges and the opportunities that globalization brings to our doorstep. Not understanding that these influences exist can lead to further misunderstandings and misjudgments, bringing out the worst of our cultural biases.

Given these cultural challenges, yet paradoxically also the inherent opportunities, this book explores how to build a more solid foundation based on the four Rs—respect, relationships, recognition, and rewards. The outcome will illuminate cultural complexities, enabling you to collaborate more productively and harmoniously with people from very different cultures. By actively seeking to develop an integrated, four-R, formulated response with colleagues from around the globe, you can proactively invite mutual discovery.

What is this mysterious four-R formula? As you will learn in this book, respect lays the foundation. Whenever someone asks to speak with you, stop what you are doing—put down that pen, close the laptop, get off the cellphone—and listen. If the timing does not allow you to actively listen, arrange a time when it will be most convenient for both of you. As you will read in this book, having the sentiment that someone has listened to you is the ultimate sign of respect across cultures. When this is accomplished, a relationship of respect is formed. In chapter 3, you'll learn about team building and coaching across cultures. Why does coaching work? Because it's based on active listening and powerful questions. These are the basic elements of building a relationship.

With these two Rs in place, you can start to recognize the other person, his or her contribution to the conversation, and his or her proposed solutions to the issues at hand. Recognition across cultures is not only about learning, for instance, that respectfully holding a Japanese business card in two hands may be expected in Japan but also a considerate gesture in other countries—because taking the time to read someone's business card when it's presented is a sign of respect. Instead of pocketing the card without any regard for the person presenting it, taking the time to look at the card and the person shows you are interested in building a relationship and recognizing the person for who she or he is—a simple gesture that can only lead to appreciation, a reward in itself.

Attentively listening to someone does not mean that you need to automatically accept the other person's input as the answer, but simply that you need to accept that the other person has an opinion that deserves to be listened to. This requires you to drop your desire to convince others of your opinion and forces you to open your mind to listening and asking probing questions. The power of a simple question—What do you think?—has more rewarding ramifications than you can imagine.

This is just a simple overview of the integrated four-R response. But putting this into action enables you to avoid reinforcing stereotypes when communication flounders, promotes an interactive relationship-oriented exchange, and eliminates preconceived attitudes as you actively engage with others from different cultures.

One important point to emphasize at the outset is that for the average worker in the 21st century, most of our cross-cultural challenges and opportunities occur right where we are—you no longer have to travel around the globe to experience a cross-cultural incident. When life is wonderful, things flow freely. There are no cultural issues in stressless environments. Yet stress is omnipresent in today's world. By having a well-rehearsed four-R response, you are able to step back when things don't seem right. Instead of a knee-jerk reaction or a nonreflective response where the outcome is one of reinforced cultural biases and stereotypes, you can press the pause button and reflect on what is happening. This moment of reflection is referred to as *cultural reappraisal*, which takes the stress out of the situation and leads to a successful interaction, especially in time of a crisis.

The Main Elements of Today's Cultural Context

In this book, I assume that you're familiar with the main aspects of globalization—and for our purposes here, in particular, how it's leading to unremitting cross-cultural experiences and dispersing workforces around the world. For more details, see Thomas Friedman's (2007) excellent book *The World Is Flat: A Brief History of the Twenty-First Century.* As the former United Nations secretary-general, Kofi Annan, noted in his opening address to the 53rd annual DPI/NGO Conference, "It has been said that arguing against globalization is like arguing against the laws of gravity."

If globalization is nothing new, what makes it such a pressing topic today? Since the beginning of time, continents have been explored, countries have been built, markets have been developed, and information has been shared across continents and oceans. Yet the concern about globalization today is now much more than fear, which, as noted earlier, has always been evoked by "alien" cultures—as in "there be monsters" on medieval maps. Today, people are heatedly concerned about the pace, breadth, and reach of incessant change (Friedman 2007).

Thus, the simple word "globalization" continues to carry with it negative implications; it has become synonymous with a threatening force aimed at changing our way of life. Will we be forced to assimilate to another culture's traditions? When does integration mean that one culture overpowers another? Earlier in this chapter, I noted the fear of acculturation—the process of adopting another culture's social patterns. If we refer to culture as an iceberg, today's globalized economic environment influences the visible aspects of culture, not the invisible or deep core values that drive people to act, react, and be engaged. It is time to rid yourself of this fear—because you can adapt to other cultures but you don't have to adopt them.

Globalization is no longer just about the world's economy. It's about the reality in which we live and will continue to live. It does affect everything—health, housing, economies, and industries—but it doesn't necessarily change everything. Sustainable change requires transformation, a bottom-up, contagious, grassroots approach—not a top-down enforced change. It needs to involve many, not few, participants. Throughout this book, I note the opportunities offered by social networking media for various aspects of cross-cultural cooperation, which are obvious when it comes to communication.

The Proliferating Uses of Social Networking Media

Social networking media obviously have both strong points and limitations. As two leading observers have noted, "Social tools are powerful building blocks that can transform the way we enable learning and development in organizations. They foster a new culture of sharing, one in which content is contributed and distributed with few restrictions or costs" (Bingham and Conner 2010, 8). In a cross-cultural context, this intense sharing can potentially lead to both greater understanding and misunderstanding.

Even though early adopters are proliferating, it is still too early to predict what influences social networks will have on cultures. The Internet may be more than 40 years old, but we need to evaluate the recent impact of the Web 2.0 applications, which have hardly been around for five years. These include wikis, blogs, podcasts, videocasts, and crowd-sourcing, along with new user-driven and community-driven interactive technologies that seem to constantly appear out of nowhere.

With the advent of social networking media, our planetary village has gone from small to tiny—with these media, we can be intimately in touch with each other always and everywhere. Time and space are receding with the onslaught of Facebook, Twitter, YouTube, and the like. The big concern is how anyone has any privacy at all—witness the ongoing controversies about the details and commercial violations of Facebook's privacy settings. Studies have tied cultural orientations of trust and information sharing to consumer use over the Internet. In countries where privacy is a value and governments regulate the amount of private information that is circulated, early adopters and trusting consumers are far and few between.

These new media also have the potential to empower people in the workplace, both individually and in collaborative endeavors, both with an intimacy and on a scale heretofore unimagined: "By equipping technicians with a media mindset and a culture of collaboration, everyone shares responsibility for educating one another and giving each person an opportunity to seek focused help. The workforce becomes the organization's lifeline to what's happening in the field right now" (Bingham and Conner 2010, 58). This underlying collaborative spirit of social networks is exactly what's driving this trend. Individual e-learning tools or training on your own, as in distance learning, have yet to prove their effectiveness. For instance, a study with implications for decision making in group settings looked at Oxford University rowers and showed that by training together, team members were able to tolerate far more pain than when they trained on their own (Winters, Pham, and Pronovost 2006).

Whatever the future implications of social networking media, the well-known "butterfly effect"—according to which, for example, a butterfly flapping its wings in Rio de Janeiro can affect the weather in Chicago—proves that our professional, personal, and educational experiences can be affected by minute, faraway happenings elsewhere in the world (*APS News* 2003). This is why you need to remove your blinders, enlarge your field of vision, and change your perspectives so you can integrate what is happening across the office hallway, across continents, and, simply stated, across the world. In practical terms, the following simple formula embodies one of the best ways you can change your perspective—where E (emotions) plus R (reaction) negatively affects O, the outcome:

$$-(E + R) = O$$

To use this formula, you must first develop a deep understanding of the invisible aspects of culture: your core values—what drives and motivates you and what triggers your emotional reactions. This is what your own culture hides from you. A total of 90 percent of the survey respondents stated that they had experienced having their values transgressed. This provoked emotions that stimulated reactions that were often beyond comprehension. And when you least expect this emotional reaction, your options or opportunities become limited.

If you have a reliable four-R response in place—given your ability to use cultural reappraisal, as mentioned above—you can recalibrate your cultural expectations and adapt them to the present cultural context. Simply ask yourself:

- Which of my core values are driving my emotional response?
- What is behind my discomfort?
- How can I shift my perspective to see the other person's point of view?
- When did this culture clash begin?
- What can I do to prevent it from reoccurring?

This process does shift the responsibility to our own shoulders, and perhaps this seems unfair. It takes two to tango, and authentic communication can only occur when it is bidirectional. When responsibility is shared and each participant gives and takes and gives again, the outcome can only be that of a high-quality conversation. Knowing that someone needs to start the process, why not let it be you? By taking the lead, you may very well persuade others to follow.

For our purposes in this book, the crucial aspect of globalization is its effect on culture—in the term of the Millennial Generation, we're living in the midst of a "mash-up" culture. What do we mean by "mash-up"? Simply the coming together of bits and pieces of popular or transient cultural aspects not native to many of the world's heretofore-distinct cultures, even though they persist and are even resurgent (witness the Slow Food movement from Italy, fighting back against the European Union's homogenizing bureaucracy).

We've all experienced this. You call your credit card company, and you're on the phone with someone in Delhi. An issue arises, and a natural reflex is to blame the incoherent situation. You open your new TV's instruction booklet, and you're dealing with a weird amalgam of English words and Korean syntax.

And this global mash-up is only just beginning. Working across barriers—cultural, linguistic, and generational—is now a reality, and even a necessity for achieving success in today's globalized business environment. Generations X and Y (and Z, in a few years) arrive at the workplace with more cross-cultural experience than any generation before them. Thanks to modern telecommunications and the Internet, they have spent time speaking with people in call centers around the world and most probably have met team players from another country without ever having left their living room or cubicle. With no actual borders, globalization is a mixing of cultures. As a Moroccan survey respondent so accurately described it, globalization is about a person who's eating Japanese sushi in an American-style restaurant and was served by an Indian waiter who's wearing French fashions (made in Morocco with fabrics from China) and drove there in a Korean car.

Findings From Brain Research

Although a detailed discussion of the findings from brain research is beyond the scope of this book, scientists continue to be surprised as neuroscience reveals how deeply culture—our language, behaviors, and values—is ingrained in our brain. What is important for our purposes here is the fact that cultural neuroscience is demonstrating how culture shapes our brain.

For example, findings from a study at the University of Alberta in 2007 compared how Japanese and American cultures interpreted cartoon and other simple images conveying a range of emotions. The study revealed that the Japanese participants (from what is known as an interdependent, community-oriented culture) focused on the backgrounds of the images and the eyes of the cartoon characters to interpret emotions, while 95 percent of the American and Canadian participants (from more individualist cultures) focused on the foreground and a single important element of the cartoon as well as on the cartoon character's mouth to determine emotions. Even when participants were shown emoticons, which are used to convey a writer's emotions in email and text messaging, similar differences were apparent. Thus, for U.S. participants, the emoticons :) and :-) denoted a smiling mouth as a happy face, and the emoticons :(or :-(denoted a sad face. Conversely, the Japanese tended to emphasize the eyes by using the symbol (^_^) to indicate a happy face and (;_;) to indicate a sad face (*Science Daily* 2007). These examples remind us how cultural differences affect global marketing and virtual team building. We may be virtually connected and globalized in our daily functions, yet we continue to conform to our culturally driven interpretations.

The importance of recent brain research is how it shows that people are creatures of comfort and habit. This affects how you need to readjust your efforts when change management or merger integration initiatives are being implemented. People have a natural tendency to find safety in similarities. To be more specific, your brain seeks out stability and familiar situations. By understanding the neuroscience of what drives human reactions, you can start to look at cultural values in a totally different light (Carter and Pelphrey 2008; Mitchell, Macrae, and Banaji 2006; Cacioppo and Patrick 2008).

For example, the images from computerized medical body scans show us how our emotions (produced by spontaneous external reactions) feed our body with internal physiological reactions (feelings). With magnetic resonance imaging scanners, these are functionally seen as blood rushing to a specific area in the brain. Physically speaking, these are experienced as an increased heart rate, heavy breathing, or sweating. Learning to redirect your thoughts and feelings—as, again, when you do cultural reappraisal—can also enable you to redirect the blood flow. Your brain's neural activity responds to your emotions and corresponding behaviors. If you understand how the brain functions when you experience certain emotions, you can become more mindful of your behavior, and thereby modify blood flow to certain parts of the brain (Ochsner 2008).

With these findings in mind, it has been said that "we are the choices we make," and scientific insights into how we make choices can illuminate workplace choices, including those affected by cross-cultural situations. Decision making occurs in the frontal lobe of the brain's cerebral cortex. As we make choices, we use different parts of the frontal lobe. For abstract decisions, we use the front portion; for concrete decisions, we use the back portion (Carey 2007). These findings are important when it comes to understanding how the brain goes from making a decision to do something to then doing it. Understanding our brain can enable us to evaluate under which conditions our decision-making process is optimized.

The Globally Dispersed Workplace

At the outset, it is very important to emphasize that given globally dispersed workforces, cross-cultural communication occurs nearly just as much for workers in place as it does for those workers who travel around the globe. This reality is clearly shown by such phenomena as weekly teleconferences, where cultural comfort zones do not always encourage active participation or when one-to-one conversations and subjective management become a thing of the past as sales forecasts are publicly shared on intranets and live town meetings via virtual videocasts.

A particularly notable aspect of this workforce dispersion is outsourcing—which is affecting highly educated and senior level employees, not just call centers. For instance, a *New York Times* story explains how large law firms are now starting to outsource their entire junior associate function to New Delhi, where the same work can be done at a savings of about 90 percent from New York or Chicago (Timmons 2010).

The usefulness of social networking media in the context of dispersed workforces is obvious: "As organizations switch to a decentralized or distributed model, transparency from company leaders is a refreshing approach that builds trust and imparts critical insights. When employees are geographically dispersed and 'walking the floor' isn't an option, companies use video to reach out in authentic ways" (Bingham and Conner 2010, 67). At the same time, cultures need time to adapt, especially when their cultural norms have been based on hierarchy and ambiguity.

Tell Me Your Story: Our Crucial Individual Experiences

Throughout this book, the individual experiences recounted in stories—told by survey respondents, colleagues in the workplace, and the like—are presented as crucially important cultural signifiers and thus as, ultimately, the embodiments of people's cultural context. Harking back to the epigraph for this chapter, these stories can both reveal and conceal people's cultural values. In this storytelling context, pertinent dimensions include indirect and direct communication styles, attitudes toward certainty and risk taking, and a sense of initiative—all of which are logically part of a person's cultural attributes. See the sidebar for a suggestive thought.

> "Having lived in five countries and having experienced four cultures intimately, I am a global nomad. . . . We need to focus on universal precepts and values that will influence humanity in a powerful way. . . . All cultures add to the mix, and we must take the best and learn to appreciate how it enriches the meaning of being human."
>
> —Saira Samee, Pakistan
>
> *How much do you agree with Saira?*

We can learn much about a culture from its legends, morals, and stories. Some cultures communicate destiny or fate as an underlying theme. In the survey used as a basis for this book, one question asked participants if they believed in predetermined destiny or self-determination. Less than the majority, 40.2 percent, believed that we consciously choose what determines our life's destiny; 48.3 percent thought their choices could influence their destiny; and 11.2 percent reported that they made choices hoping that they were aligned with a predetermined destiny (figure 1-1). Cultural stories laid the foundation for these respondents' beliefs—beliefs that are now influencing perceptions, value determinations, and communication.

An example of this is in a story recounted by a French client who was invited to a wedding in Mumbai. The country general manager was marrying his daughter. Even though Marie-Christine (the French vice president who had hired the general manager) had not planned to attend the three-day wedding, local employees made it quite clear that she had little choice but to attend. When she arrived at the wedding, the general manager introduced her to many of the guests by saying that it was only due to luck that he was able to marry his daughter today. The day he had met Marie-Christine more than seven years ago, his stars had been aligned. His future and success were guaranteed. Without Marie-Christine, nobody would be at the wedding today. At first, Marie-Christine had thought he was joking or that perhaps she hadn't understood his English. When she realized that he was perfectly serious in introducing her in such an important way, she remembered how astrology, fate, and destiny played an important role in Indian culture.

Another example when destiny or fate is an underlying factor is often heard during interviews in Hong Kong. When I asked a future employee to explain why he thought he was a good candidate for the job, his reply surprised me. He first explained that he was the oldest in the family. Then he went on to show me the jade bracelet that his mother had given him for the interview. This was meant to bring luck. After all, I did hire him, so perhaps there's some truth to underlying beliefs.

When proverbs and sayings from one culture are analyzed, and also compared with those of other cultures, they can often reveal similarities or differences related to a basic cultural message, such as learning the importance of perseverance. For instance, the often-cited American proverb "Where there's a will, there's a way" explains how Americans learn to overcome external forces. Not only does this reveal the underlying individualism behind the drive of self-initiative, it also sets the stage for a culture of calculated risk takers.

Likewise, the American saying "If at first you don't succeed, try, try again" is impossible to translate into French. The idea of making several

Figure 1-1. Destiny or Determination?

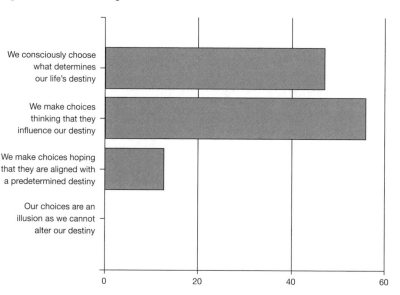

mistakes before succeeding is a very American approach to risk-taking. A more common proverb in French translates as "no matter how small it is, a failure is always a failure" (*aussi petit soit-il, un échec reste un échec*). Proverbs do influence mindsets. Attitudes toward job security in France and in other countries demonstrate that lack of risk-taking and initiative can be linked to fear of failure.

Whatever the underlying themes in these learned proverbs and stories, they do provide us with a pair of cultural lenses. By looking through these lenses, we can learn to develop a worldview. How we adjust these lenses enables us to receive, perceive, and conceive the stories that give meaning to our lives.

When you are actively involved in a story, every nut and bolt of your perception is utilized in the process—verbal and nonverbal language, as well as the whole range of emotions that influence thoughts, moods, and feelings. In telling and hearing stories, people come together to engage in an exchange of expressions, ideas, images, and information. As they listen to a story, each person starts to interpret what he or she is hearing according to his or her own history and expectations. People give meaning to situations, expect outcomes, and develop context based on their past experiences and cultural influences. Therefore, when serving as a narrator, you need to be attuned to the listener. You are reaching out and touching his or her mind in hopes of connecting and communicating a message. This act, in itself, requires you to use both your head and heart, and your thoughts and emotions, to move, empower, and engage the listener.

To illustrate this reality, let's consider the story of one of my French clients, whom we'll call Emmanuel. When companies choose people for international assignments or global teams, their concern about how to show respect toward others is key to successfully working in today's global workplace. Yet, as more and more companies go through the globalization process, they adopt generic core values, often with an Anglo-Saxon bias, expecting the people in their foreign operations to abide by them. Confusion, tension, and misunderstandings are often the result. This was the case for Emmanuel.

During a meeting to define stakeholder goals for a coaching contract, Emmanuel's boss and his human resources representative explained that to be successful, Emmanuel needed to become more affirmative, more direct, and more of a risk taker. During this discussion, I saw confusion spread across his face. And even more than confusion, there was an internal conflict of values surfacing from deep within.

In a coaching session, with the help of a simple list of cultural values (see worksheet 2-1 in chapter 2), Emmanuel chose those that resonated the most for him—relationships, modesty, cooperation, and reputation. Just reflecting on his choices and comparing those to the stakeholder objectives, he understood his emotional discomfort at the earlier meeting. His cultural values were not aligned with those of his stakeholders. Before the end of the session, he defined the behaviors he associated with the values he had chosen and those the company was asking him to develop. At the end of the session, we reviewed how he planned to put the stakeholder feedback into action and how he could find a balance between remaining authentic with respect to his own values and meeting the company's objectives. These kinds of cultural values are what give meaning to our lives. They are those guiding principles held deep within us until they surface, often unexpectedly, when behaviors provoke emotional reactions.

As experience shows, a person cannot be told what cultural values to live or work by. As adults, we need to discover for ourselves which values are our priorities. There are many ways to learn about those values that influence you the most; but if you want to look more deeply into the values that have influenced you over your lifetime, a more advanced research tool is available from Values On Line (www.valuesonline.net). The developer of this tool and CEO of Values On Line, Jan H. Mattsson, emphasizes the importance of a self-discovery process that can enable you to find your authentic self. You are the only one who truly knows who you are. Your everyday behaviors, attitudes, decisions, and perceptions of others are based on values you have chosen as priorities—your core cultural values. Over time, with experience, maturity, and circumstances, these values can change based on your different life stories and experiences. And keep in mind that values and behaviors are very much a chicken-and-egg dilemma—whichever precedes the other, both are intimately intertwined and interdependent.

Toward Understanding Today's Cultural Complexity

In the end, culture comes down to everyday behavior—the choices you make in the situations you face. I could go on and on about the challenges of dealing with cultural complexity in today's workplace, but it will be more useful here to share a simple tool I developed for the survey I conducted in 2009: the Cultural Framework Survey, given in worksheet 1-1.

Worksheet 1-1. Cultural Framework Survey

Choose the statement that best describes your preferred attitude, behavior, or assumption. There are no right or wrong answers.

1. Rules or situations:
   - Rules should be adhered to at all times.
   - Rules are guidelines adhered to whenever possible.
   - Rules are written for the sake of having a basic understanding.
   - Rules are made to be bent.

2. Individuals or groups:
   - Individual recognition and rewards are motivating.
   - Individual recognition and rewards can be detrimental.
   - Individual recognition and rewards provoke jealousy.
   - Individual recognition and rewards go against human nature.

3. Caring for others or competing against others:
   - We must take care of those who cannot fend for themselves.
   - We should give a helping hand to those weaker than ourselves.
   - We can all keep an eye out for those in need.
   - We need to look after ourselves.

4. Thought processes: get to the point or get the meaning:
   - It's important to state only the essential facts.
   - It's preferable to give some context to the facts.
   - It's essential to give the full context to define the facts.
   - It's the context that reveals the essential information.

---

5. Destiny or determination:
- We consciously choose what determines our life's destiny.
- We make choices thinking that they influence our destiny.
- We make choices hoping that they are aligned with a predetermined destiny.
- Our choices are an illusion as we cannot alter our destiny.

6. Information sharing:
- Information should be shared openly whenever possible.
- Information should be shared in doses to avoid overload.
- Information should be shared with only those concerned.
- Information is only valuable if shared at the right moment.

7. Risk taking or cautiousness:
- Risk taking is the essence of innovation.
- Risk taking requires accurate calculations.
- Risk taking necessarily includes a fear of failure.
- Risk taking is dangerous.

8. Emotions: to show or not to show in public?
- Emotions should only be shared in private.
- Emotions should be carefully controlled.
- Emotions should be expressed in a healthy manner.
- Emotions show commitment, empathy, and passion.

9. Time: limited or limitless?
- Time is precious and needs to be accurately managed.
- Time is manageable and best if well managed.
- Time is tough to manage, and we never have enough of it.
- Time is what you make of it.

10. Who you are, or who you know?
- I am who I am because of what I achieve.
- I am who I am because of my determination to achieve.
- I am who I am because of what I have achieved in the past.
- I am who I am because of what my family has achieved in past generations.

Using this survey, look at your own preferences. The survey's 10 simple questions cover learned behaviors and expectations. There are no right or wrong answers. They seek to get at your feelings about adherence to rules, individual recognition, mutual responsibility toward others, communication styles, decision making, information sharing, risk taking, emotions, time, and reputation. By being aware of your behavioral preferences, you can become aware of the behaviors that would seem foreign to you or may be a source of underlying irritation for others.

Worksheet 1-1 can help you see the basic assumptions that underlie your particular culture. In my experience with this tool, its simplicity helps to get the conversation going. Reflecting on circumstances as organizations go through the globalization process, we discuss the challenges of implementing standardized policies and procedures. In cultures where situations tend to override company policies, complaints of "it depends" and "things are different here" are often heard. These stories reveal situational preferences. Whatever the tendencies, the challenge does not come from how, but when, to implement company policies and procedures.

I have often heard people say that rules will be respected if they are respectable. When was the last time a company policy seemed absurd to you? Does standardization improve situations or constrain creativity? The small/medium/large approach has never gone over well in countries where haute couture and exceptions to the rule are more often in fashion. When it comes to individuals and group orientation, pay for performance and team motivation are jeopardized. Knowing how to find the balance in these simple statements first means that you must remove the "or" and replace it with "and." Only then can you take each statement and decide to what extent it is helpful or detrimental to the corporate culture.

R R
R R Questions for Reflection and What's Next

This chapter's key points include the complexity of culture and the importance of context. The added value is conveyed by what our differences bring to the table, and how our values motivate us and inspire us. Now consider these questions:

- How would you react when interacting with someone whose answer to a question on the Cultural Framework Survey (worksheet 1-1) is completely different from your own?

- What kind of learned behaviors might be in conflict when you meet and interact with those from another culture? How can you overcome these?

- How could you see the Cultural Framework Survey as helping with a particular cross-cultural challenge you face in your organization?

In chapter 2, you'll find a deeper explanation of the importance of respect, the first R. You'll learn how to engender respect and especially how to develop it for yourself in a cross-cultural context. This is where we start to lay the foundation for the four-R response. You'll learn to manage the stress that comes with working across geographical, cultural, and linguistic barriers, not to mention time zones and generations.

Chapter 2

Respect in the Cross-Cultural Context

Words like "freedom," "justice," and "democracy" are not common concepts; on the contrary, they are rare. People are not born knowing what these are. It takes enormous and, above all, individual effort to arrive at the respect for other people that these words imply.

—James Baldwin

What does it mean to respect someone or something? When trying to understand a complex reality like "respect," it's helpful to look at the word's etymology. The word "respect" is from the Latin *respectus*, which literally means "regard," with the sense of the "act of looking back at one," and the past participle *respicere*, meaning "look back at, regard, consider" (thanks to Douglas Harper's *Online Etymological Dictionary*, www.etymonline.com).

This "act of looking back" connotes a person making a conscious effort to turn around and take a moment to think of—consider—what has just been said or done. In doing so, the silence that follows gives the speaker the feeling of being heard, truly listened to, and appreciated while giving the listener the time to choose the best response. In the workplace, when you are confronted by an unfamiliar cross-cultural experience *and* have learned to master this simple gesture of respect—attentively listening, integrating what you have heard, and considering alternative options, instead of shooting from the hip—you exercise restraint and think before you speak. In workshops facilitated around the world, when I ask participants how respect is shown in their culture, they unanimously agree that having the impression of someone truly listening to you is the ultimate sign of human respect.

The word itself, "respect," resonates with everyone. Without going much further than the local shopping mall or workplace, think about how much you show respect in your own daily exchanges. You can also think of examples of when others fail to show you respect: the little slights, disrespectful remarks, or uncivil behaviors that occur every day with shopkeepers and colleagues. According to the book *The Cost of Bad Behavior: How Incivility Is Damaging Your Business and What to Do About It* by Christine Pearson and Christine Porath (2009), U.S. companies lose millions of dollars a year through loss of employee effort, teamwork, individual turnover, and missed opportunities due to incivility. Disrespect unconsciously affects people's focus and ability to work.

Whether in the living room, dining room, or boardroom, respect may very well be the universal answer to the question: How do we communicate more effectively with or without cultural and linguistic barriers? Knowing that attentive listening means so much to people around the world, what prevents you from answering with "yes" when someone enters your office and asks "Got a minute?" The consequences of respect and disrespect run high risks locally and in our everyday lives. One can only imagine how valuable this simple gesture of listening is in the globalized arena of the workplace, where we constantly work across cultures.

The Context of Working Across Cultures

Instead of trying to flatten the world with identical behaviors, beliefs, and assumptions—or defining differences in tidy, sterile boxes—you need to learn about and respect cultural differences, while also being true to yourself. To maintain this authenticity, you need to expand your comfort zone and define behaviors inspired from around the world, not only values from within. When it comes to respect, being culture savvy is about "accepting that you're going to work with people of different cultures, and that not one culture is going to dominate," as Andrew Gould, chairman and CEO of Schlumberger, stated in a McKinsey interview in April 2010.

How is respect portrayed in today's globalized, intercultural context? Behaviors can vary widely, according to our cultural assumptions, but contemplating what respect means is human nature—see the sidebar.

For instance, being too informal can be misinterpreted as being disrespectful, something all cultures despise. It is not to say that being charismatic is an unappreciated personality trait when meeting new people or finding your bearings in unfamiliar environments. The ability to put people at ease and draw on every human being's desire to be accepted and recognized for who they are, is definitely a plus when it comes to melting the ice. But why "melting the ice," as opposed to "breaking the ice"?

Let's consider an example. While I was running a team-building activity with a group from a recently merged company, there was some discussion on how arrogance was portrayed. A German we'll call Dieter described the first time he had met his new American colleague, Jim. After strolling into Dieter's office, Jim grabbed a seat, swung it around,

---

Here's a vignette from an international assignee: "When I first went to live in the States, I was pleasantly surprised by the sense of wide open spaces and friendliness. In the neighborhood we lived in, children played out in the street in the cul de sac, the yards had no fences and people were always willing to lend a helping hand. I couldn't understand why it sometimes bothered me as my kids' friends came running through my house, calling me by my first name, and opening the fridge to get something to drink or eat. I felt like they were invading my privacy, my space. When my neighbor first invited me over for coffee, I almost felt a jolt of lightning when she said, 'Help yourself. The cream is in the fridge.' I was paralyzed. I couldn't imagine opening this woman's refrigerator. It sounds foolish but it was true."

In which ways is this story about value systems? How can we show respect if we don't question our learned behaviors? What are our assumptions? How can this person relieve her feelings of disrespect and relive this experience differently?

and leaned back into the chair, in a slightly off-balanced manner. He put his arms out and his hands folded on his head as if he were stretching. "Hi, I'm Jim the new director of marketing. I thought I'd pop around to introduce myself to some of the people around here." Dieter stared at him, thinking: Who does he think he is, strolling into my office, taking up my time with a big welcoming grin on his face? Nobody has introduced us.

Dieter felt that Jim was being arrogant—to be so at ease in someone else's office was somehow showing a lack of respect, the epitome of arrogance. Later, Jim laughed as he heard Dieter recount their first meeting. Jim's impression had been entirely different. He had gone to Dieter's office to be friendly and, as he said, to break the ice. It seemed everybody in the German office was addressing each other as Herr Doctor this, Herr Doctor that. The formality was cold, reserved, and palpable. Jim just assumed that because they were all on the same team, some friendlier, informal attitudes could build up the team morale. That's when he learned that Dieter's apparently standoffish behavior was actually the cultural norm. Having been raised in a protocol-driven, status-oriented culture, the workplace was for working and one's private life was for friends not colleagues. Many of Dieter's colleagues were getting accustomed to the American use of first names, but when speaking in German between colleagues, they continued to use surnames and titles.

A similar occurrence took place in France, while I was facilitating a cross-cultural expatriate workshop. I mentioned that the French don't tend to socialize with colleagues after work. The division between a person's private life and public or professional life was very distinct. The two participants—Wendy, a British woman, and Susan, an American—were surprised. Being used to happy hour drinks between colleagues and pints at the pub back home, they even explained that their French colleague, Philippe, who had recently returned to France after having lived in Britain for several years, went out for drinks with them at least once a week. We attributed this to the fact that he had been an expat, so he was familiar with British social customs.

The following week, they told me that when Philippe invited them out for drinks, Wendy and Susan answered that their department director,

Mary, was in Paris visiting from New York. They had invited her to join them for drinks. Much to their surprise, Philippe was a bit taken aback and explained that he could go out for drinks with his peers but definitely not with his boss.

As is shown in this case, attitudes toward hierarchy, equality, and the private and public (professional) spheres are found well below the visible tip of the cultural iceberg. These learned behaviors based on assumptions and beliefs remain invisible, even to ourselves. They are accepted and hardly ever questioned—it's just the way we do things. Because these subtle differences were discussed during the three-day workshop, Wendy and Susan were at ease discussing this with their colleague, Philippe. Learning what each person had assumed to be the respectful way of including or not including the boss consolidated their relationship as they discussed what respect for equality and privacy meant to each other. Thus, culture became a part of the conversation and not a scapegoat or an uncomfortable avoidance.

Humans all over the globe feel the need for respect in both personal and professional environments. To know what might be considered impolite or a "mistake" in another country, the future expatriate or international team player must delve into his or her basic cultural assumptions, beliefs, and values—and not necessarily seek to acquire other people's habits. Learning about one's own expectations and values reinforces respect across cultures.

Other examples of respect and disrespect include ways of learning about but not necessarily adopting the stereotypical behaviors from one country to another. The risk is simply immense success or utter failure. For instance, in September 2003, Starbucks chairman Howard Schultz said in a statement that "it is with the utmost respect and admiration for the café society in France that we announce our entry into the market" (Ryan 2003). The French reaction was utter surprise. Newspapers glared with headlines: "Could French Philosopher Jean-Paul Sartre Have Found Inspiration Sipping from a Paper Cup of Steaming Starbucks Java?" Coffee is a centuries-old experience in France, and many traditions—like a small cup of espresso in smoky bistros with grumpy service from bow-tied garçons—die hard.

Knowing that Starbucks would have to face up to a hard-edged French slur against watered-down coffee like the kind found in many U.S. diners known as *jus de chaussettes* (juice wrung from soggy socks), Schultz's audacity was more than risky. Any cross-cultural trainer might very well have advised Starbucks not to venture into such a culturally infested mine-field. Yet, in January 2004, it dared to open its first smoke-free café in a city where close to four out of 10 people smoke. Against all the advice about formal French attitudes, coffee cashiers announced orders ready to pick up by calling out first names written on paper cups while jazz music and smiling faces welcomed the long lines of caffeine-craving customers. Instead of laughing Starbucks out of town, customers flocked to the new café.

In explaining the Starbucks' success, Schultz noted, "We are not in the coffee business serving people but in the people business serving coffee." Isn't this the ultimate sign of respect—listening to customers' needs; greeting people with warm, open hearts; and tending to the emotional connection with consumers. In coming years, this and other stories of cultures clashing will become a familiar one as Starbucks and similar multinationals expand their global presence. Thus, in May 2008, Starbucks brought Paris to Taipei with the launch of Starbucks Discoveries Paris Chilled Cup Coffee—a chilled cup of cafe au lait, which is the first of its kind in the Taiwan market.

It's important to note here that these kinds of cultural exchanges are not unilateral. For instance, in July 2010, fast food giant McDonald's reported a 4.6 percent growth in second-quarter sales in the Middle East region, with sales of fish sticks and oriental-style vegetarian pita wraps at the top of its menu offerings. The question "Where's the beef?" takes on a totally different meaning as globalized companies adapt to the local cultural context.

As younger generations are more and more connected through social networking media and satellite television, they become more open to new experiences. Their cultural expectations are based more on a human experience than a traditional one. For social artifacts, the future of France may very well be going toward a Starbucks culture.

Does this mean that the French, Chinese, or Korean cultures, to name a few, are in danger of disappearing? Once again, we can look to the impact of social networking media to get a better understanding of what is taking place and how these media will affect respect for national cultures in the years to come. In response to a question posted on a social network site in October 2010, my colleague Alex Ma shared the finding that in China, these media have introduced a Western life style to more and more Chinese families in the city, and many young people have adopted or formulated lifestyles from different cultures but know little about their own culture. Recently, however, China made big improvements by setting up Confucius Institutes all over the world to teach the Chinese language as well as introduce Chinese tradition and culture. Koreans are doing OK with this issue of using modern social networks to introduce and promote their own culture, but meanwhile the government is emphasizing preserving cultural traditions and historical interest, not only to let their own children get familiar with their culture but also "export" their culture abroad. These are examples of social networks working in favor of exchanging cultural views, and not imposing only Western viewpoints.

Paths to Cross-Cultural Respect

Having looked at respect overall, let's consider the main paths to respect among employees in a cross-cultural context. One aspect is learning to pay attention to each other's stories. The morals behind our culture's stories affect us monumentally. They leave us with images, notions of good and bad, and feelings of right and wrong—the basis of our values, which form our beliefs. As explained in chapter 1, one of the best ways to get to know people is to hear the stories they have been told and those they tell themselves. But to be able to listen to other people's stories with open minds, you need to first examine the stories you hold true. When you learn to objectively understand how your culture's stories have influenced your values, beliefs, and perceptions, you can then begin to receive and analyze another's story. You can begin by asking yourself:

- Which stories from childhood influence my actions?
- What was the moral, the metaphor, the meaning being communicated in the story?

See the sidebar for two stories and reflect on how they might influence a cultural perspective.

When stories are infectious, they have the power to change people's attitudes, motives, and behaviors. Yet to do so, your interpretations of stories (and the other paths to respect) need to take into consideration the particularity of the cultural situation. Beyond the intricacies of a story, there are other methods of communicating simple, yet powerful, messages.

A Story from the United States

In *The Little Train That Could* by Watty Piper—a popular children's story in the United States—a small engine agrees to pull a long, heavy train over a steep mountain to deliver toys to the children on the other side of the mountain. The engine struggles to climb the mountain and, in the process, watches all the fancy new trains passing him by. The little engine keeps repeating out loud: "I think I can, I think I can." The toys that he is pulling chant encouragements, "You can do it." And in the end, despite adversity and challenging circumstances, the little engine does do it. He pulls the train to arrive safely and happily to the other side.

What does this story tell us about values like determination, independence, results orientation, and altruism? How might this story contribute to an American "can-do spirit"?

A Story from India

A survey respondent, Hari Iyer, contributed this story about Dharma. While crossing a flooding river, a sadhu (an Indian mendicant) saw a scorpion drowning. He tried to save it by picking it up and putting it on safe ground. But the scorpion stung the sadhu's hand, he jerked it away in pain, and the scorpion fell back into the river. But again, the sadhu tried to save the scorpion. A person standing on the bank of the river observed this pattern and asked the sadhu why he didn't just let the scorpion drown. He answered that the scorpion's dharma (that is, its basic characteristic or duty) is to sting, while his dharma is to save. If the scorpion, even in the face of danger, did not abandon his dharma, how could he—a human being—abandon his?

How might an Indian from Bangalore react to self-initiative? What kind of emotional reaction might an American with a "Where there's a will, there's a way" attitude have when working with someone who relates to his or her dharma or fate as an ingrained value?

For instance, metaphors are one-sentence stories, which, if well designed, have the ability to touch hearts and minds. The context in which they are used shapes the frame of reference for the listener. The meaning behind a metaphor can provoke deep-rooted emotions and images.

Let's consider a metaphor. While speaking with a client who had recently arrived in France from Hungary, I asked him to describe his integration process. He simply stated, with eyes alight: "I feel like I am just starting to learn to play the violin, in public, and I want so much to be part of the symphony orchestra." If you have ever tried to play the violin, you can imagine the painful scratching of the bow against a string as you learn to apply the right pressure. If you have never tried to play the violin, or any other musical instrument for that matter, the image of being a lone player and wanting to be part of something bigger might have more significance for you.

Context and experience drive meaning. Through stories and metaphors, we reveal values, beliefs, and assumptions. For this Hungarian, his difficulty in finding the right words was like trying to find the right cords on a violin and applying the right pressure to empower his team. Those attempts brought back memories of his childhood experience, when he had learned to play the violin. Had this newly arrived manager not been able to define these inner feelings through this metaphor, his frustrations would have remained his own. But by humbly communicating his desire to succeed and find the right way to inspire those around him, he was able to touch their hearts and build the trust that became the turning point in the newly formed global team searching for cohesion. Because every human experiences life through different contextual lenses, being able to fine-tune your story and not force your perception on others is a step toward becoming culture savvy. How have your stories helped or impeded successful communication?

The book *Kiss, Bow or Shake Hands*, by Terri Morrison and Wayne Conaway (2006), reviews protocol and behaviors on how to adapt to, but not necessarily adopt, respectful behaviors. The book helps readers understand the gestures, history, and ethnic differences within countries. Behaviors have meaning and associated stories that are specific to a cultural heritage. Values are derived from the stories we are told, and the stories we tell ourselves. Lists of dos and don'ts ignore authenticity and inform you about preferred actions—not behaviors. Respect is shown through how you behave, revealing the values you hold within.

Disrespect, on the other hand, is defined as treating someone with contempt or rudeness. When this occurs, those external, spontaneous emotions that turn into long-lasting feelings are tied to our values and how we perceive ourselves, at that time, in that situation. The feeling of having our values transgressed can be particularly painful. In the survey I conducted in researching this book, 83 percent of participants recognized the experience of their values being transgressed; see figure 2-1.

Figure 2-1. The Results of the Survey Done for This Book

Choose three to five values from the list below that are a priority for you.

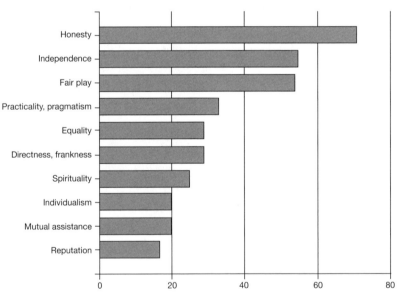

Have you ever experienced a situation where you felt that someone had transgressed your values?

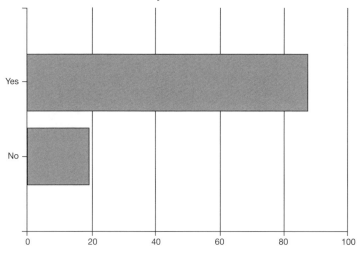

If yes, which emotional response did you feel?

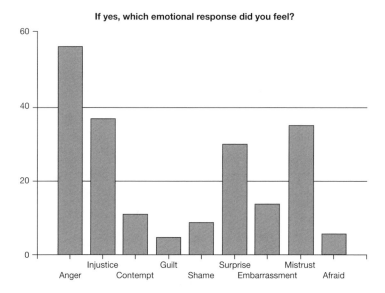

A major step forward in building bridges across cultural divides is admitting the emotional reaction that occurs when you sense that your cultural values are being transgressed. Understanding that these emotions rightfully exist allows us to let go of them. Imagining that we can just suppress them will only allow our frustrations to erupt at a later date—and reinforce an "us-versus-them" stereotype. To see how complex values can be, try worksheet 2-1. And then consider the results of the survey done for this book, given in figure 2-1.

Worksheet 2-1. Cultural Values List Exercise

From the following list, choose and, if possible, prioritize four or five values and eliminate two or three values that are not a priority. Describe a behavior that demonstrates the values chosen:

Tradition	Innovation	Recognition
Patience	Passion	Generosity
Accountability	Loyalty	Initiative
Cooperation	Competition	Privacy
Openness/directness	Efficiency	Material possessions
Consensus	Fun and enjoyment	Honesty
Independence	Family ties	Formality
Informality	Reputation	Power
Modesty	Security	Relationships
Risk taker		

Referring back to the introductory discussion of authenticity, review your personal expectations:

- What values drive you?
- Which values do you look for in others?
- How would you have reacted if you were the "new" friend trying to make yourself at home—comfortable helping yourself to the cream in the refrigerator or not?
- Where do we draw lines between private and public domains?
- How deep are our expectations between formal and informal behaviors as predetermined conditions for respect?

Learning and Practicing Respectful Communication

Having looked at the complex relation between values and feeling respected, it's time to consider how you can best communicate respectfully in the globalized, multicultural workplace. Communication is the process of sending messages, receiving information, and feeding it back within a context. When this context includes culture, as it inevitably does, things start to get complicated.

The foundation for learning to communicate respectfully is becoming aware of the stories we live by—and acquiring the ability to question the validity of these stories in today's global context. During our formative years, our parents, caretakers, teachers, heroes, and, later on, corporate mentors influence our sense of distinguishing between the right way to do things versus the wrong way. Over time, through many kinds of stories—proverbs, lessons learned, and sound advice—our brains become hardwired and learn to react a certain way when faced with certain dilemmas. The feeling of "that's just how it's done around here" describes this gut reaction—the heartfelt sense of knowing right from wrong. But can one culture be right and another wrong? As you probably learned from the cultural framework exercise in chapter 1 (see worksheet 1-1), the answer is a resounding *No*.

Growing up in different cultures means that everyone is hardwired differently and has different ideas about how to do certain things. This inevitably causes conflict when business goals and project deadlines are imminent. By developing transcultural sensitivity, you can learn to integrate different perspectives and solve problems synergistically yet competitively. This is what empathy is all about. In becoming more empathetic, you move away from focusing on cultural differences and toward cultural convergence. This enables you to view the value that each culture brings to the table. It is not about cultural assimilation, whereby one culture overrides the other, but more about taking what works best in each culture and building a functional third culture.

As globalization becomes an integral part of our everyday existence, we are starting to see shifts in what were once considered country-specific cultural behaviors:

- In those countries where rules were too flexible, compliance is key.

- In those countries where ambiguity reigned, clarity in communication is emerging.

- In those countries where time was adaptable, schedules are being reinforced.

These changes in behaviors are just the by-products of a flatter world where information is exchanged in nanoseconds. Looking at how these behaviors may become ingrained will show us how we can possibly devise a third culture—one that works for all involved. In fact, research in neuroscience is revealing how the brain records actions and responses by mirroring the behaviors of people in our environment. Despite the controversy of these recent discoveries, learning certain behaviors appears to incite specific reactions. Mirror neurons, as they are called, are very active during the first 12 months of a baby's life and may influence language acquisition as well as what is considered acceptable behaviors in a certain cultural context. Researchers at the University of Parma have published findings that revealed the same brain cells fired when a monkey watched humans or other monkeys eat a peanut as when it ate a peanut itself (Rizzolatti and Arbib 1998). They called these brain cells "mirror neurons" because they reflect the action of others.

Growing up in the United States, I remember learning proverbs that taught me behaviors that were valued, such as "Actions speak louder than words" or "Where there's a will, there's a way." This repetition and constant exposure is how values are developed. Then, as happens to many of us during one of those trips abroad or while working in today's globalized workplace, we are confronted with situations in which the "right" response based on our ingrained values is now perceived as disrespectful or as inappropriate. My learned behavior of spontaneity, for example, may conflict with my client or co-worker's need for thoughtful reactivity (perhaps based on his or her values of security, tradition, formality, and reputation), and I may get frustrated.

The good news is that this reaction is physiologically normal. As first described in a study about stereotyping and how the brain reacts with familiar and unfamiliar faces (Hart et al. 2000), we learn that we are social beings looking for compatibility and cohesion. Studies reported by scientists reveal that our brains become hardwired through our life experiences and develop a sense of expectations as a means of survival (Ochsner and Lieberman 2001). When what we encounter does not fit into our norm, the initial reaction is one of internal conflict, as in "That is not what I have learned to be the 'right' way of doing things, so it must be wrong." These reactions may very well be the foundation for our cultural biases. Some people refer to this experience as *culture shock*; today, it is commonly described as "brain shock," the brain's reaction to what is unfamiliar.

Thinking back to my story about Emmanuel in chapter 1, we can understand that his initial reaction of misunderstanding was directly tied to his interpretation of the story—in this case, the objectives—to which he was listening. At my next coaching session with Emmanuel, I found him once again stretching his comfort zone, but not in ways I had imagined. He was pleased to announce that he had become much more affirmative, had been tracking specific actions he had taken, and would even be able to include these new behaviors in his upcoming individual development plan. Then the confusion appeared once again, with him saying "I don't think the guys on the team really appreciate my new attitude."

Having already looked at the cultural values and issues arising from contextual situations, we now needed to look at how Emmanuel and his team were creating a new story in tune with the changes happening and the underlying tension since an American investment group had acquired the French company six months earlier. The newly implemented behaviors seem to have run amok. Questions during our coaching session had Emmanuel reflect on the expectations from his French peers:

- How might being more affirmative be seen as disrespectful?
- How was risk-taking behavior perceived?
- How do you show respect with a more direct communication style, especially in a culture that values indirect communication in a hierarchal context?

Training workshops gave Emmanuel the tools to apply and measure success in the change management process, but it was through encouraging reflection with powerful questions and ongoing coaching that he discovered the deeper meaning of what being an authentic leader is all about. The executive coaching enabled him to question his ingrained "right" and "wrong" values and adapt his behaviors to bridge the cultural divide between what people at the United States–based headquarters expected and what was contextually feasible in the French corporate culture.

At the same time, Emmanuel was able to integrate what at first appeared to be incoherent behaviors conflicting with his desire to be true to his core values while finding culturally acceptable behaviors that would enable him to reach his and his stakeholders' goals. He learned to be affirmative while preserving relationships. He is now a calculated risk taker who understands the importance of the lessons-learned process. His communication style is more direct and based on clarity, while integrating the need for formality and protocol. By surfacing awareness, understanding value-driven behaviors, and talking about the stories being told since the acquisition, he was able to shift perspectives and exceed objectives. In the end, his successful project launch proved that he could find coherence in conflict and build respect across culturally preferred behaviors.

The Challenges of Communicating Respectfully Across Cultures

Communicating respectfully across cultures involves a number of challenges. You have seen how behaviors and values define respect, and how culture influences the stories that shape your worldview. In this section, you will learn about the complexity of communication, the differences between explicit and implicit communication, and how to break down the barriers between cultures. You will then be able to bring culture into mainstream conversations. Your takeaway tool for improved communication will be understanding how to balance "advocacy" and "inquiry," as described by Peter Senge, Art Kleiner, and Charlotte Roberts (1994) in *The Fifth Discipline Fieldbook*. No matter which culture has influenced a part of who you are today, key competencies for showing respect include the art of listening, the ability to be solicitous of others through inquiry, and storytelling.

Communication Is Complex

A 1998 *Wall Street Journal* article found that for 480 companies surveyed, communication was considered the most valued interpersonal skill. Done correctly, it is also one of the most difficult to learn. As is true in storytelling, communication goes beyond the simple, one-way sending of messages. William Isaacs' book *Dialogue and the Art of Thinking Together* (1999) states that when conversing, most of our time is spent preparing what we want to say when we should be simply listening to what is being said.

Clear, unbiased communication is hard. Communication goes well beyond written and spoken words. How we are perceived, the context in which a message is sent, and the attuned environmental changes all contribute to the complexity of communication. All these elements are part of communicating across cultures. To make it more effective, you, as the speaker, need to check that all the information, emotions, interpretations, and ideas are conveyed as intended. Through open-ended questions beginning with "what," "how," and "when"—but never "why," because "why" often provokes a defensive reaction—and the use of appreciative inquiry (a positive, forward-thinking approach to future possibilities), you invite the listener to comment on what he or she has understood.

As the listener, you need to question your expectations and interpretation by reformulating what you have heard, not by preparing your answer while listening to what is being said. You cannot hear another person if you're thinking of your answer before his or her sentence is completed. What is being said will only be perceived as noise while you are actively searching your brain for your self-centered reply. To determine which questions or answers may lead to misunderstandings originating from the use of language and the influence of culture, you need to remind yourself that communication is necessarily a two-way street.

A fundamental characteristic of being *culture savvy* means being aware of how your communication style may be perceived by others. Understanding your own cultural expectations, being at ease in discussing them, and proactively apologizing for possible misinterpretations should, over time, allow others to be comfortable in joining in on the conversation. Learning to always take your business outcomes seriously, but never taking yourself seriously, is the first step toward breaking down cultural and linguistic barriers.

Without this knowledge, the most well-crafted communication fails to get its message across. Effective intercultural communication is based on active listening and focused attention, as well as the communication tools of balanced advocacy and inquiry (see the sidebar).

Advocacy and Inquiry

How can you effectively communicate when you need to find the balance? The steps you can follow to bring clarity to cross-cultural communication are based on balancing inquiry and advocacy, as described in *The Fifth Discipline Fieldbook* (Senge, Kleiner, and Roberts 1994, 253-259). Knowing your own communication style (indirect versus direct), and then distinguishing between and balancing advocacy and inquiry, effectively bridges cultural and linguistic divides with respectful communication.

Advocacy is what you are often taught to do within explicit communication styles—argue strongly for your point of view and be a problem solver. It is based on the approach that says "Here's what needs to be done, what I need from you, and asking for your input on what is *my* idea," which a listener can interpret as being rather one-sided, especially those more familiar with an implicit communication style preferring consensus and active listening. If you want a dialogue, an exchange between at least two people, you want to invite brainstorming, which is asking others to make their thinking process visible. So instead say something like "Walk me through what you are thinking about" or "Describe the situation."

By balancing both advocacy and inquiry, you remove power and positional posturing and replace them with platform discussions. This type of dialogue gets below the surface, beyond the ego conflicts to shared underlying interests. It combines multiple perspectives. A nice way to balance the two is by giving context to advocacy: "Here's what I think; here's how I got there. What do you think?" By adding inquiry, you reverse the one-way process and demonstrate respect for the individual—and thus show that you value what the other person is thinking.

People accustomed to hierarchal and power positioning may, at first, be taken by surprise that their boss or elder is asking for input on a situation. Reassuring them that their experience and knowledge are valuable eases the tension and recognizes the person for who they are—a human being who wants to contribute to a better outcome for all involved.

Often, your role when communicating and collaborating is to clearly get your point across while empowering co-workers and teammates to be valid contributors to the dialogue. The following steps can help you do just that. If you don't know the person well, start with step 1; otherwise, go directly to step 3:

1. Make your thinking visible. Clearly state your objectives or reasons why the conversation is taking place: "I need some clarity on this week's progress report on project XYZ."
2. Wait for the other person's undivided attention. Explain why you need it and why it is important that you get it. Brains don't multitask, even if we pretend that they do.
3. Recognize your own communication style and give context. If you tend to be direct, let the other person know up front: "I don't want to be perceived as aggressive, but finding some solutions for the delay would really relieve the pressure I'm getting from HQ." "Sorry to be so direct, but clarifying where we are today and where we will be by next week will be very helpful."
4. After stating assumptions or conclusions, invite brainstorming and multiple perspectives by asking others to make their thinking visible: "What do you think?" "How do you see this differently?"
5. Meet the other person's level of energy or emotions by acknowledging them: "I can see this is upsetting for you" or "You seem to be very excited by this opportunity."
6. Focus on open feedback with a preference for feed-forward—that is, not dwelling on what went wrong (the past) but considering how to build on and improve on what is going well (the present and future): "What else can be done?" "How else can you get what you need?" "Who has a suggestion about how we can turn this situation around?"

These steps bring cultural behaviors and interpersonal styles to the forefront, making them a part of the conversation, engaging all involved to share and collaborate, inviting innovation and creativity to the dialogue, and underlining the mutual desire for effective communication.

Explicit and Implicit Communication

Research on the importance of context across cultures was first done by Edward T. Hall, as reported in his 1976 book *Beyond Culture*. He described cultures as being "low context" (explicit/direct) or "high context" (implicit/indirect). A decade later, Lennie Copeland and Lewis Griggs, in their book *Going International: How to Make Friends and Deal Effectively in the Global Marketplace* (1986), put cultures into a spectrum of levels of context, showing that Germans, Americans, Scandinavians, and English Canadians were considered low context, while French Canadians, the French, Italians, the Spanish, Mexicans, Greeks, Arabs, the Chinese, the Japanese, and Koreans were increasingly higher in context.

In general, lower-context, explicit cultures feature informal behaviors and tend to be less hierarchal and more welcoming of foreigners. This is often the case in countries with a past steeped in international trade, linguistic and cultural diversity, or high influxes of immigration. These characteristics are indicative of today's global economy. In higher-context cultures, protocol or insularity influence the level of implicit communication. The very fact that implicit means implied—understood, though not directly expressed—lays the foundation for ambiguous situations when the people communicating do not share the same understated experience.

Survey participants shared some of their own experiences of cultural assumptions, expectations, and implicit communication. Jonathan Rice—a partner in JNH Rice Associates, a cross-cultural business consultancy based in Kent, England—explained how it took him a long time living in Japan to understand the value of consensus. There were many conflicts along the way. One day, his secretary told him "You are so decisive." It was the biggest insult he had ever received! In Japan, consensus building is a highly valued cultural belief—rooted and reinforced through childhood stories. Taking the initiative to suggest a solution without consulting others is seen as totally disrespectful, an uprooting of the belief that decisions are made in harmony. This example illustrates the challenge of communication—learning to be explicit, beyond words, by understanding cultural values and belief systems.

Unfortunately, communicating is not as easy as just choosing to be more implicit or explicit. It goes well beyond the simple choice of words.

Nonverbal communication is even trickier. For instance, the common hand waving learned in North America as a way to greet someone is used to say goodbye by those who speak Farsi, the official language of Iran. Shaking the head from left to right means "no" in some countries, but in other countries, especially India, it is considered a means of accepting what is being said, almost agreeing. When entering or leaving meeting rooms, the hand-shaking ritual is often a sign of respect with implicit meanings—who shakes whose hands, why, and when?

Breaking Down the Barriers Between Cultures

So how can we break through the barriers we build when miscommunicating across cultures? We need to make a conscious effort to not only question our expectations but also voice them. How can we do this in ways that are not perceived as disrespectful? This is where the influence of globalization is a positive guiding force. By learning about cultures, the taboos of misperceived cultural behaviors become part of the conversation.

Imagine the scene the morning of the second day of an intercultural workshop where laughter filled the room. The participants were greeting each other with handshakes, bows, bear hugs, and cheek kissing. When we can talk about what had once made us uncomfortable, we become curious. Our interconnected world has countries and cultures questioning their habits and choosing between what they like elsewhere and leaving behind what they don't like within their own learned behaviors. Those cultures known for their implicit or indirect communication styles are seeking clarity, and those known for directness are catching the PC fever—political correctness that tends toward avoiding discussions. When change is in the air, the pendulum often swings from one end to the other before finding its midpoint.

Another barrier found with conflicting styles of cross-cultural communication has to do with how information flows. When styles conflict, this can trigger emotions. A feeling of unfairness—a sense of being blindsided when information is not shared in the expected manner, either overtly or often too late, when it could or should have been shared proactively—now becomes the focus of what went wrong. Information that stagnates leads to power pockets, with in-groups and out-groups. Rumor mongering and backstabbing are side effects of poor information flow. What solutions can be put into place to get information flowing at a desirable level?

When clarity and purpose are priorities, effective communication is the central focus. An example of this came out during a workshop that turned out to be more about resolving communication effectiveness than specific cross-cultural issues. The workshop theme was communicating across cultures. The participants were three human resource directors from the United States, Germany, and France.

The American and the German tended to fall into the free-flowing, information-overload category, sharing proactively and copying almost everyone on their email exchanges. But their French counterpart leaned toward a filtered flow of information by trying to solve issues before she involved everyone. So she limited her email exchanges and did not want to bother her colleagues with unessential problems until they were solved internally. At the same time, she was totally overwhelmed with the amount of email, in English, that she was constantly receiving from both her colleagues. Her American and German counterparts believed she was being "sneaky" by not sharing up front, while she felt they were inundating her inbox with things over which she had no control. Being conscientious, she dutifully read and reread all the emails, thinking they were expecting her input, when actually they were just keeping her "in the loop."

The issue was simply solved by establishing email subject headings—"For info" or "Request for action"—an easy solution to what had developed into an emotionally draining experience for all involved. Setting down guidelines for corporate email protocol and Netiquette (email and Internet etiquette) is essential to remove the ambiguity when choosing who, how, and when to copy on emails.

If you know that your communication style is considered very direct, learn to adapt it to the receivers. Recently, a workshop participant emailed me his needs assessment questionnaire without any greeting, just the words "file attached." I was not surprised to read his answer to the question concerning his communication style: "Colleagues have told me I am too direct and perceived as impolite." But I was shocked to see that he had obviously done nothing to rectify this perception or his rudeness. Sending an email without the slightest acknowledgment to the receiver is not a sign of directness; it is a lack of basic recognition—the third R in the four-R formula for working and collaborating around the world. "Hello" and "thank you" are easy to type and not too time consuming.

Techniques for Communicating

Now let's take into consideration three essential elements required to successfully communicate across cultures. Here are some overall, helpful reminders:

- Expect that communicating across cultures requires more time and more patience.

- Listen more than you talk, which allows you to observe the nonverbal behaviors.

- Be attuned to and comfortable with expressing acknowledgment of the emotional and personal involvement you bring to the discussions; this prevents building frustrations from miscommunication. Meet others at their level of emotions by recognizing their right to express their emotions.

- Invite others into the conversation through inquiry, which shows respect for opinions and people.

The first element is that communicating across cultures requires courage. As much as communication across cultural and linguistic barriers is difficult to decode without a cultural mentor, expecting and accepting these challenges are what makes it all the more interesting and rewarding.

Second, it requires integrating two different thought processes. Understanding communication styles also requires you to try and understand various thought processes. In general, those with the tendency toward low-context, direct, and explicit communication styles have a high respect for the use of time. Their pragmatic approach will often have a "get to the point" or linear pattern to speaking—an "actions speak louder than words" attitude. They start with the overall desired result, give the facts that support it, and draw up action plans and conclusions. This is known as inductive reasoning, sometimes referred to as the bottom-up approach, in which the starting point of the discussion is with the expected result. Specific observations are collected from others, which leads to specific data confirming the previously announced result or objective.

Others start with a general theory, then make interconnected relationships between or beyond the facts and figures. Referred to as a top-down approach, or deductive reasoning, this process goes from specific observations toward broader generalizations and theories. Deductive reasoning starts with an observation, and the next step in this logic might involve attempting to find things that disprove the assertion, with hopes of enlarging the debate and eliminating contrarian observations.

An example of these divergent thought processes provoking a cultural misunderstanding is that of an American national making a presentation to her European counterparts. When introducing the new project along with the desired result, the American tends to expect that the others listening will give constructive suggestions for moving the project forward toward the announced result. The Europeans, however, have been taught strict critical analytical skills, whereby they think their role (as the listener) is to voice each and every way in which the project could stall or fail. This deductive approach is meant to enlarge the debate, but the American's perception is that these people are mean-spirited and negative. The Europeans' perspective is that by exhaustively trying to find fault with the project or proposal, they have done their due diligence and have eliminated the possibility of failure. If their several attempts to find flaws are unsuccessful, and the presenter is consistent in her view of the project, then the proposal is validated and has been properly vetted. The European team will then most likely give their full buy-in. The American, however, is sure to feel frustrated, defeated, and wary of her European teammates if she is not aware of this cultural expectation.

How can you alleviate this situation? Once again, it is not about adopting foreign ways but understanding that we need both approaches— a specific, to the point, results-oriented, and factual inductive thought process as well as a circular, interconnected, and theoretical approach. Not knowing that both approaches can coexist is what destabilizes us. If innovation and imagination are missing from your team's discussions, try inviting both thought processes to the table. Much like the tool described in Edward de Bono's *Six Thinking Hats* (1985), which structures the thinking process in a detailed and cohesive way, you can use the approach of alternating inductive and deductive reasoning. The process consists of these steps:

- Be explicit about the outcome.

- Empty your thoughts of all that is negative or possible detrimental elements to the successful outcome.

- Now that your mind is clear and negativity is out on the table, your analysis can avoid paralysis, which comes from not verbalizing what could go wrong.

- Use divergent thinking, which opens up all the possibilities as absurd as imaginable.

- Apply convergent thinking, which draws out the realistic possibilities and leads to consensual conclusions.

- Then go for it!

For an illustration of how these various factors come into play, see the sidebar.

Third, get comfortable being uncomfortable. At the beginning of a cross-cultural training session, when there are both native and nonnative English speakers in the room, I often ask everyone to introduce themselves in their native language. This causes a certain stretching of comfort zones for some Americans, who assume that English is the company's language and that it is a waste of time to listen to the contributions in a language other than English. Those who are nonnative speakers consistently thank me for allowing them to show that they are fluent in another language and to have Americans get a taste of what it is like to not necessarily understand all that is being said.

Why waste precious time in incomprehensible introductions? Because our native language has the ability to make thoughts visible,

Handling the Elephant in the Room

An example that brings to light these thought processes and communication clashes was told to me by a British executive. During a crucial meeting with his multicultural team, he explained that the problem they were dealing with could be referred to as the proverbial elephant in the room. Pointing to the closed door at the back of the meeting room, he announced to the 10 people seated around the table that no one could leave the room until a solution was found.

In this approach of breaking down the problem, the discussion was meant to move from the general issue to specific solutions. The British executive started by announcing "Let's take this elephant by the trunk" and then went on to dissect the elephant, using it as a metaphor for solving the problem. After removing the imaginary elephant's trunk and ears in the problem-solving process, three of the participants in the room had obvious difficulty keeping themselves focused on the problem. When asked why they weren't adding to the discussion, they almost broke into laughter when one of them answered "Your elephant is a mammoth"—in other words, the problem was now larger than when the discussion had started.

These three team members looked at problem solving from a synchronous, interconnected perspective. They did not break things down into manageable items but built things up to get an overview of the entire issue by asking themselves "How does this problem relate to or influence other issues the team might encounter?" By enlarging the debate, the team could get a bigger picture of the problem's seriousness. This is a sensory approach based on intuition and a feeling for the problem, as opposed to reducing the issue at hand to a linear, checklist approach. Research shows that when both approaches are optimized, the multicultural experience enables people to solve structured problems with a higher success rate and with increased creativity (Jia, Hirt, and Karpen 2009).

By giving both a big-picture view of the outcome and a specific step-by-step approach to the problem-solving process, we have a thorough evaluation with multiple perspectives. It takes more time at the outset to include each cultural perspective in the problem-solving process, but the result is usually worth more, with long-lasting buy-in as well as long-term savings of time and money.

to generate distinctions, and to voice opportunities and optimism. The choice of words we use, the humor we share, and the complicity of how we engage with each other are intimately tied to the language we use to express these emotions and ideas. As second-language speakers, many foreigners state that they speak English fluently, but when faced with native, monolingual anglophones, they lose confidence in this fluency. What is obvious and evident to those who share a common language may not be to others.

Fear of creating the wrong mood or energy, and of not choosing the right word that expresses the accurate emotion, leaves many English-as-second-language speakers hesitant to openly participate. Feedback about foreign colleagues—such as "lacks charisma" or "appears to be a slacker"—are common from anglophone, monolingual peers. Linked to the same misconceptions are remarks that foreigners tend to be negative. When hearing those comments, foreigners often retaliate by explaining that they are modest realists, not superficially supportive. The intonation and choice of words may influence the different perspectives of the same situation. Issues related to ineffective decision making or action taking at the end of multicultural meetings often have more to do with the lack of being able to integrate the decision-making process into their native language than with the need to get hierarchal buy-in.

Allowing colleagues the time and space to recap decisive issues among themselves in their native language often promotes quicker buy-in. These are just simple gestures of respect, and they often become the basis for developing trust in relationships, which is essential in building our second universal value, relationships (discussed in chapter 3). See the sidebar, and try writing a six-word memoir.

R R / R R   Questions for Reflection and What's Next

Before considering a few questions for reflection, let's look back at what's been covered in this necessarily longer chapter on respect. This chapter has shown why, the next time someone says to you "Let me tell you a story," you should let the person do so. Remember that expectations

---

Write a Six-Word Memoir

To write a six-word memoir or metaphor is quite a challenge, but if well done, it can be rewarding. Inspiring others requires the interpersonal skills of a good communicator. Part of this is being able to share experiences and stories that challenge ideas or that convey empathy with others. Now that you know that values form the foundation of culture and how your stories can reveal your beliefs and assumptions, use what you've learned by writing a very short story of your own. This exercise is based on the story that Ernest Hemingway's colleagues bet him that he couldn't write a complete story in just six words. When he wrote the following, they paid up:

For sale: Baby shoes, Never worn

By having a message that tells you and those around you what gets you up in the morning, how your behaviors are seen in the greater light of enabling others, who you want to influence, and how you expect to do so, will give your life a deeper meaning and an inspiring message for others to follow. Mine might be summed up somewhat like this: "Bridging divides—better lives—flatter world."

---

play an important role in the clarity of respectful communication and relationships. Getting comfortable while being uncomfortable is what crossing cultural and linguistic divides is all about. By letting down your facade of unexplored expectations, you learn to be more welcoming of others, more curious about their life stories, and more engaged in your own. While listening to the stories we tell ourselves, or those that are told to us, we must keep an open mind, a curious and attentive focus on what is being said or left unsaid. This is the first step toward entering into the conversational dance of life. When given the time, this is what makes stories so enjoyable and, in turn, shows respect and builds trusting relationships. Our stories and life experiences influence our perspectives and how we are perceived.

Now that you have learned how you expect behaviors based on your cultural orientations and how you tend to assume story endings based on your experience, you need to change. As was shown in chapter 1 in the Cultural Framework Survey, worksheet 1-1, people are "different" because:

- They are more individualistic or group oriented.

- They appreciate rules and regulations more than the exceptions to the rule.

- They need to share ideas openly or only by sharing in one-to-one or in small, private spaces.

- They believe in being a caring society versus a competitive one.

- They have an inner drive to succeed and to take risks compared to a more fatalistic view where they accept that they can not necessarily influence the ways of the world.

As this worksheet shows, being aware of how our choices and how words and behaviors influence those around us are the first steps toward integrating cultural differences and becoming culture savvy.

Differences will remain negatively different if we look at others within this frame of mind. Learning only about differences may lead us to develop mental models that we then go out and seek to confirm. Accepting that cultures are dynamic systems, and that each person rightfully comes to the table with the added value of being unique, opens the door to welcoming others with curiosity, respect, and the desire to break down, not build, barriers. By learning to listen to the stories we tell ourselves and others, we develop active listening—communicating beyond words with images, gestures, and meaning that every human heart is more open to understanding. To develop a narrative that reaches out to others, start by assessing the emotional climate. Be explicit, emotional, and empathetic. Don't assume the happy ending, yet keep a positive, realistic outlook. When this is done, authentic rhymes with inspirational; listeners are easily engaged.

The stories that successfully cross cultural and linguistic barriers are based on the four-R model—starting with respect for oneself and for others. This can never be one-sided. The "You get what you give" syndrome is ever more prevalent when we give respect through verbal and nonverbal empathetic resonance. As stated above, showing respect does not necessarily require us to adopt procedural salutations originating from age-old customs of status, hierarchy, and formality. Being aware of how we address others makes us mindful of possible misperceptions of rudeness. Understanding the risk of adopting foreign behaviors without understanding the depth of the cultural implicit values connected to the behavior can be harmful to building long-lasting, trusting, and meaningful relationships, especially as we meet and greet others in the same room, each with his or her own cultural specificity.

This is not meant to say that we should avoid partaking in local customs, but to remind us of the need to delve below the simple gestures. Authenticity is about being true to ourselves while being attuned to the needs of others and the environment in which we find ourselves. With our flattening world, we are starting to see mannerisms leading toward an integration of preferred styles. Due to greater geographical distances, and the technologically shorter time it takes to send and receive messages in today's interconnected world, there is an increased desire for clarity in communication. Social networking media are changing the way we interact, with whom, and for what reasons. Even in countries known for their implicit communication styles, we read every day how governments, companies, or people in the streets are asking for more transparency in policies and decision making.

As the world becomes more and more global, we all need to reflect on the importance of clarity in our communication and transparency in our thoughts and actions. The simple act of greeting one another has taken on a culture of its own, as we see both a quick hug along with a handshake or a peck on the cheek as forms of adapting to various international methods of salutation. Expanding your natural comfort zone, understanding each others' stories, and avoiding judgment when taken by surprise are part and parcel of integrating cultural patterns. Just like globally manufactured goods, where all the components come from various countries of origins, it seems that the direction in which our world is taking us is finding a balance between preferred behaviors and communication styles with various countries of origin. This sign of the times—integrating, not overriding, preferred ways of showing respect—is the key to successfully yet respectfully crossing cultural and linguistic barriers.

Now consider these questions:

- How do our values influence our behaviors when showing respect?

- Where is the balance between our preferred behaviors, as revealed in the cultural framework given in worksheet 1-1 in chapter 1, and our values, as discussed in this chapter? What about those of others, our friends, family, and colleagues?

- How well do the stories and metaphors we tell travel across cultural and linguistic barriers?

- What meaning do others interpret from our stories, intentionally and unintentionally?

- How effective is our communication style when crossing cultural and linguistic barriers?

This chapter has focused on the first universal cultural principle, respect, which is put in practice by showing interest in other people, their history, their background, who they are, and what they stand for. Active listening, attuned awareness, and open curiosity with a humble beginner's mind will break down cultural and linguistic barriers. Chapter 3 explains about reaching out to others in search of developing relationships, the core to a meaningful life. You'll see that the second universal principle, relationships, is more than universal—it's human. Whether through kinship or friendship, we all need to be needed. To what extent may vary, but wellness and balanced lives find meaning in helping others.

Relationships: Team Building and Coaching Across Cultures

A human being is part of a whole, the "universe." Our task must be to free ourselves from the delusion of separateness.

—Albert Einstein

Relationships are at the heart of crossing cultural barriers in the workplace. Bringing people together, forming connections, and influencing stakeholders and stockholders all require the ability to break down barriers and build strong relationships. In particular, team building and coaching embody the key importance of relationships.

This chapter consolidates what you've learned about the art of listening while looking at the art of conversing and focusing on how to build teams and effectively coach people. How do you influence others and build trust? Is it through focused one-to-one conversations, flexible time orientations, or political correctness? As I noted earlier, science has shown that we are social beings. When you walk into that room full of friends and foes, your sensory system seeks out the friends and rejects the foes. Getting beyond your initial reactions and moving toward building trusting relationships is not only a sign of success but also one of happiness. And this is true across hallways, continents, and cultures.

But before we get into the details of how to build relationships, try an exercise to identify your comfort zones, given in worksheet 3-1. Where are your comfort zones?

Worksheet 3-1. Your Comfort Zones: Being Efficient or Effective?

Identify your comfort zones with this scaled questionnaire by rating your level of agreement on the basis of 1 to 8. Choosing 1 shows that you do not agree; choosing 8 shows that you are in total agreement.

I feel at ease in foreign environments where people do not speak my native language.

1 ___ 2 ___ 3 ___ 4 ___ 5 ___ 6 ___ 7 ___ 8

I find it easy to mingle and get to know new people at international conferences.

1 ___ 2 ___ 3 ___ 4 ___ 5 ___ 6 ___ 7 ___ 8

I take the time observing who knows who before initiating projects when new on the job.

1 ___ 2 ___ 3 ___ 4 ___ 5 ___ 6 ___ 7 ___ 8

I enjoy discussing a variety of subjects over a lengthy meal.

1 ___ 2 ___ 3 ___ 4 ___ 5 ___ 6 ___ 7 ___ 8

I can let go of judgment easily when I encounter behaviors that are surprising to me.

1 ___ 2 ___ 3 ___ 4 ___ 5 ___ 6 ___ 7 ___ 8

I observe my environment before taking decisive actions or conclusions.

1 ___ 2 ___ 3 ___ 4 ___ 5 ___ 6 ___ 7 ___ 8

I think one-to-one/face-to-face meetings get better buy-in than general group meetings.

1 ___ 2 ___ 3 ___ 4 ___ 5 ___ 6 ___ 7 ___ 8

A score of 45 or more shows characteristics of someone with an expanded comfort zone. Compare your ratings with those of your friends and colleagues.

The comfort zones identified in worksheet 3-1 illuminate the themes of how to build relationships. By rating your level of comfort in these situations, you build self-awareness, which leads to self-confidence. When you know how comfortable you are in foreign environments and crowds, you are not surprised by feelings of isolation or oversaturation. If you are not accustomed to being surrounded by people who speak foreign languages, fatigue sets in as your brain actively searches for familiar sounds. If you are a nonnative English speaker participating in a conference where English is spoken all day long, your brain becomes saturated, often making you feel overwhelmed. Mingling requires you to make the most of small talk—not easy for people who prefer one-to-one conversations. Developing keen observation skills is essential as you work around the globe, or locally. These skills enable you to quickly discover who the influential people are in certain contexts and when decision making needs to be decisive or consensual across cultural and linguistic boundaries.

In my experience using worksheet 3-1, I've seen people go from cringing in fear to adventurously seeking out relationships. I've used this tool in group workshops where participants divide up into smaller groups according to their shared level of comfort. When you find yourself in a small group of peers who share your feelings, you open up and can easily discuss emotions. The smaller groups then ask the other groups how their behaviors are perceived and explain how they would like to be perceived. Simply knowing that others had mistaken your behaviors as arrogance or aggressiveness is enough to get the conversation going so you become less judgmental the next time you find yourself needing to expand your comfort zones. For another example, see the sidebar.

You can become more comfortable with the challenges of building relationships across cultures—by expanding, not just stretching, your comfort zones. It does require letting go of comfortable ways of doing things, dropping facades formed over the years, and taking the risk of making a mistake. When it comes to forming multicultural teams, the stakes may be higher because everyone is required to break down barriers and expand their comfort zones. But the benefits are even more bountiful.

During a coaching session, a Swiss German woman executive in London explained how her discomfort at not fitting in quickly dissolved as she ventured out and tried to be less judgmental by agreeing to participate in events that she would never have done had she been "back home" in Zurich: "I had arrived in London over a month ago when my colleagues invited me to join them for 'a girl's night out'—something I had never done back home. We all met at a local bar-restaurant for happy hour at 5 p.m. Cocktails were two for the price of one, and there was finger food in plates set out around the bar. At first, I was surprised when my glass of wine arrived, filled to the rim. After a while, I was able to let go of my preconceived ideas and got into the habit of balancing my appetizer plate, drink, and handbag. I really enjoyed the conversation and friendly exchanges—it was actually great fun! I finally felt a sense of belonging—and that this adventure, coming here to live in a foreign country, was going to be successful after all."

Relationships and Cultural Norms

The subject of relationships and cultural norms is complex. Let's consider some of the more important aspects:

- How can you understand socialization patterns?
- How can you discern the difference between expectations and projections?
- How can you understand the role of perception in relation to expectations and communication?
- How can you understand communication patterns?
- How can you deal with political correctness?
- And finally, how can you move beyond communication—to foods and friends?

Understanding Socialization Patterns

Dissecting the socialization patterns of a culture will help you more fully understand what the people value. The cultural dimensions that refer to relationship-oriented versus task-oriented cultures often have more to do with family obligations and social norms than with a work ethic.

Relationship-oriented cultures with strong family ties don't usually socialize with co-workers after office hours, as seen in the example in chapter 2 about the French, British, and American colleagues. Relationships are most often built during the time spent at lunch or around the coffee machine. If this is the case, conversations can cover a vast array of subjects, yet business matters are usually left to the side. After lunch, many people from Latin-influenced cultures and countries often linger over coffee. Time-pressed Americans or British nationals—being more task oriented, and used to building relationships during happy hours or after work on weekends— feel the need to return to the office. This is a cultural mistake. The window of opportunity to build a relationship has just been slammed shut without the slightest inkling why. This point is illustrated in the sidebar.

The Cost of Not Building Relationships

A French executive recounted this story when her firm's new British account manager was transferred to the regional office in the South of France: "We would arrive at the office every morning around 9:00 a.m., and he was already there, telling us proudly that he was an early riser and liked getting to work by 7:30 a.m. Then, when we all went for coffee a little past 10:00 a.m., we would invite him. Once again, he would smile nicely but say he didn't drink coffee. He showed us his bottle of the local mineral water, already half empty. He thought he was integrating the team by drinking our local water. Little did he know that he was insulting us—from showing up at the office very early before normal office hours to refusing to join us for coffee. He said he had work to do, but many of us thought he was probably snooping in our files and reporting back to headquarters on our being inefficient. The mistrust was palpable. When he would leave for lunch at noon, we all laughed. It wasn't meant to be mean; it was his total lack of awareness that shocked us into laughter. Where did he go for lunch at noon? Restaurants didn't start serving before 12:30 in France. And to think this British executive had turned the office around in Japan! What had he done, replaced all the Japanese by British robots?"

Just as you learned with comfort zones, if this "successful" British executive had developed better observational skills, he would have noticed that nobody arrived before 9 a.m. and nobody went to lunch at noon. If he had been more self-aware, he would have had more self-confidence and could have shared his anxieties of not fitting in. The result may very well have been an expanded comfort zone and some high-quality cross-cultural conversations.

Many well-intentioned, efficient (task-oriented) Americans are surprised when they first encounter the leisurely lunches or lack of working lunches in many foreign countries. The feeling of wasting time creeps up on them after 45 minutes of sitting in the company lunchroom. Suddenly—with a friendly smile, a quick wave, and an "I'll meet you all upstairs" remark—they are gone. Little do they realize that business discussions are saved for the moment when sipping a small cup of coffee allows for digestion to set in and contemplation to begin. Time spent just listening to people—to their concerns, their interests, and their level of commitment—is time well spent. Across the globe, face-to-face and one-to-one meetings outside meeting rooms speed up the buy-in process by getting information to flow freely, breaking down hierarchal barriers, and breaking through the ambiguity or political correctness often found in meeting rooms.

The gradual building up of a relationship starts with these small steps of spending high-quality time together. Even if your idea of efficiency is based on time being saved, wasted, or used at will, when it comes to relationship building, a good reminder is that it takes time. When the investment is ripe, the relationship becomes the foundation for building trust. This is why relationships are an essential part of becoming culture savvy.

Assuming that group-oriented cultures (a cultural dimension often used to describe the Chinese) need little supervision and work well together will quickly lead you to frustration as turf wars, hierarchy, and high-context (implicit) communication styles come to the forefront. Erroneously expecting people to break the ice easily, and to accept a team-oriented, business-first approach to relationships, may appear to be efficient in the short term but is highly ineffective in the long term.

The key to relationship building across cultures is understanding these social norms. When my clients discuss the challenges of team collaboration and cooperation as they try to align multicultural and virtual global teams, there is often an imbalance between being too task oriented and not enough relationship oriented—being too concerned with being efficient and not enough with being effective. Finding the balance between tasks and relationships and between hierarchies and flat matrixes is the challenge we face and will continue to face in global organizations. These are also the opportunities you can seize to create a success story of building a third culture, where everyone identifies with what works best for all involved when roles, responsibilities, and relationships are brought into focus.

Let's again consider the British executive described in the sidebar above who was so successful in turning around the company in Japan. Once he had succeeded in Japan and had been promoted to France, he thought the transition would be easy. After all, what could be so different? As it turns out, a lot had to do with his expectations. Our British executive's idea of being respectful was slightly confused with efficiency. He would arrive early, get on with his work, take short lunch breaks, and be friendly—not much in the way of relationship developing with those behaviors. This efficient, results-only-oriented work ethic may have been the reason he was successful in Japan but not in France. His interpersonal style didn't work with *la vie à la française*, and, ultimately, he ended up leaving the company.

This British executive's lack of relationship building wore him down. In retrospect, he admitted to not having entertained many relationships while efficiently working in Japan. He was there to do a job and do it well. Company objectives and personal goals were what drove him. Arriving in France with another language to adapt to and the challenge of again turning around a company through restructuring and layoffs were certainly energy draining. His behavior of "going it alone" may at first have been a natural reaction of self-protection. Unfortunately, he was perceived by others as cold and uncaring, which only made the task at hand that much more difficult.

The gap between how this British executive was perceived and what he had expected was enormous, and so was the cost. In the end, a relaxing lunch with a colleague or two might have been the make-or-break moment he needed. It would have enabled him to tune into the seasoned employees' issues and share empathy while still reaching goals and expectations in the allotted time. Instead, he left with burnout, and the company needed to replace him. The cost was well beyond financial— relationships to re-create, reputations to revive, and going back to nine months before this well-intentioned British executive arrived in a country that he thought was closer to home.

Expectations Versus Projections

The differences between your expectations and what you actually project in a given situation can have a great effect on your ability to build relationships with your colleagues. Knowing that, when overused, your strengths can become your weaknesses, you need to rely on the stop–listen–look approach of developing observational skills. Far too often, you arrive at a new workplace or on a new project team with the objectives in mind, assuming that everyone new to the team shares your goal-oriented convictions. The time-pressed, achievement-oriented person is obsessed with getting up to speed and celebrating some small wins within the typical 90-day cycle. This determination overrides the time needed to develop relationships for buy-in and sustainable engagement.

When it comes to moving to a foreign city to manage a project or team, it is common to assume that the farther away a country, the more difficult it will be to adapt. Also, it is common to assume that the shorter the assignment, the easier it will be to handle. Cross-cultural training is often prescribed for those who are sent on long-term assignments and to countries perceived as a totally different culture than their own.

Experience is showing that when you assume that "everything will be just fine," your brain goes on automatic pilot (its preferred mode), preventing you from being attuned to subtle underlying differences of perception and communication styles. By not questioning your expectations, as seen in the example of the British executive or time-efficient Americans, you have no idea of how others perceive your projected verbal and nonverbal behaviors. Friendly, informal, efficient manners may start with good intentions, but are likely to be interpreted differently when the context calls for more formal behaviors or a relaxed scheduling of time.

In cultures where words like *mañana* or *inshallah* mean that time is perceived as being totally flexible and out of one's control—your well-intentioned behaviors may project the opposite of what you had intended. Adopting a "this will be very different" attitude opens your mind—and thus your sensory system—enabling you to be more attuned and more welcoming toward others, which in turn enables you to adapt with more ease. Willing your brain to be aware of reactions and interactions as you try to build those relationships is the very meaning of being open-minded.

Understanding that there will be unexpected emotions and unforeseen needs for better coping mechanisms is what resilience is all about. Taking the steps from being self-aware to questioning your expectations, and to accepting different perspectives, requires that you learn to understand that others will perceive your behavior differently. Knowing that what you expect and what you project may very well be left up to the beholder better prepares you for the adventure and allows for an appropriate cognitive adjustment.

Perception, Expectations, and Communication

But what is perception, after all? It's the stimulation you receive from incoming information through your sensory system (your mind) being compared with thoughts (cognitive, brain-based processes) that come from your past experiences, worldview references, and learned behaviors. The messages being sent and received stimulate a personal, physical, and physiological response of acceptation or rejection. A high level of self-awareness helps you find ways of coping with these often-uncomfortable contradictions. You can learn to be more effective—and more accurately calibrate expectations—by developing a sharper perception of who you are, not only your strengths but also your blind spots of how you may be perceived by others.

Knowing how you are perceived when you interact with others is an important layer to a more solid foundation for relationship building. In the discussions thus far, we have built our foundation of understanding who we are, what motivates and drives our behaviors. The next step is to take this knowledge and transfer it to your interactions. This transition—leaving behind your nonreflective accepted self and going forward with a newer, more promising acceptance of an authentic self—takes courage. This is transformation.

To be transformed, you need to reflect on not only how you communicate your underlying values, beliefs, and assumptions but also on how your very perception of these preferred behaviors reflects your attitudes toward others. As was learned with the Cultural Framework Survey (worksheet 1-1 in chapter 1), you have preferred behaviors, thought patterns, and communication styles. Whether it is a direct, get-to-the-point style with measurable objectives (task focused) or an indirect, context-oriented, emotionally expressive style (relationship oriented, with some lingering over lunch), you can see how these preferences affect how you build relationships. The way you perceive time—is it a usable commodity or a relational experience—will influence how welcoming you are of others.

The following questions can help you get to know yourself better by determining how far the pendulum swings when choosing between these extremes, and how others might see you when you behave in this manner:

- During working hours, is "just getting something done" a priority over taking time for a friend or colleague?
- When in doubt, is my fallback position compliance over context—one where rules and regulations are accepted over people and situations?
- Do I prefer direct communication, transparency, and openness over the time-consuming ambiguity of giving and saving of face?

One preference is not necessarily better than the other. And contextual situations matter. But in all cases, understanding that perceptions and expectations clearly lead to effective communication is what learning to be truly intercultural is all about. Clarity does not need to be direct, rude, or without propriety. Relationships are based on communicating with respect, listening with intent, and reformulating with curiosity.

For a more thorough assessment of cultural preferences, the Cultural Orientations Framework is a tool that facilitates the understanding of salient cultural characteristics for individuals, teams, and organizations. This tool, which is based on Philippe Rosinski's groundbreaking book *Coaching across Cultures* (2003), goes hand in hand with an inclusive and dynamic vision of culture, beyond the traditional binary and static approaches, which often tend to reinforce stereotypes.

Understanding Communication Patterns

As you build diverse relationships with friends and colleagues across the globe, communication goes well beyond just the styles you have learned about up until now. Communication patterns take on an entirely different form with the onslaught of virtual communication. As researchers have observed, "Computer-mediated communication technology is becoming the backbone of many organizations, supplanting the formal hierarchical structure to achieve coordination and manage relationships within and between organizations. Electronic communications fuel the growth and effectiveness of an organization and its parts. Information, rather than being limited, controlled, and a source of power, appears to be instrumental for greater effectiveness when widely disseminated and freely available in so-called virtual electronic organizations" (Daft and Lewin 1993, iv).

Yet how is this effectively changing communication patterns? With colleagues spread around the globe, or telecommuting from wherever and whenever, the global workplace is geographically decentralized and time zone dispersed. Email and phone calls are the means of communication that tie virtual teams to each other and to the organization. What is written takes on a life of its own as social and cultural contexts are left for interpretation. As other researchers have noted, "E-mail messages have been found to contain high socioemotional content" (Wiesenfeld, Raghuram, and Garud 1998). This explains why being culture savvy is essential in today's global workforce. Intercepting the written word with an angry word, or judging the tone when a colleague chooses to use more formal wording or long-winded explanations—all will inevitably lead to miscommunication.

To avoid this miscommunication, you need to look at the patterns of communication that affect how people build relationships in a workplace involving constant cross-cultural contacts. When "I heard what was said, but what did he or she mean?" provokes a gut feeling of being misunderstood, an internal alarm should go off. A reminder that it is once again time to reevaluate our assumptions and expectations. By tuning into the immediate environment, we can observe how people interact in their native language with compatriots. Often, the image of a sport may come to mind. The perceivably polite manner of "I speak; I pause. She speaks; she pauses," exchange has been referred to as the tennis-serve method.

Often, a comfort zone for British English speakers, combining the ill-fated tag sentence with the tennis-serve exchange, falls flat when crossing linguistic barriers. The "nice weather, isn't it?" question starts with a description and ends with an invitation to the listener to add their own comment, in hopes of starting a conversation. Unfortunately, 9 out of 10 times, a foreigner politely answers with a blunt "yes" or "no." Period. End of conversation. That's of course if the polite British person was able to enter into the conversation.

While reviewing evaluations from a workshop, I was surprised to see an executive from Britain give a very low score to the French presenter. Her knowledge and mastery of historical and contemporary events were usually highly appreciated. When I asked why, he looked surprised and replied, "She was so impolite. I couldn't get a word in edgewise!" That's when I realized we hadn't discussed communication patterns across cultures.

Having been influenced by listening habits and thought processes that incorporate concepts of space, time, and complexity, this British executive was obviously more comfortable with the well-timed tennis serve, as described above. In Continental Europe, he was more likely to be immersed in the volleyball conversation, where everybody jumps in before the end of the speaker's sentence to carry the ball or conversation further.

Try asking for directions on a bus in Italy, Spain, or Mexico—before you know it, most everybody has a comment to add. The jumping into the conversation is a sign of enthusiasm and interest. And, of course, there's the famous fencing style of the French. In fencing, the opponent is never there to stab you in the heart, but just to provoke a reaction. In France, the speaker knows exactly when to stop "provoking" to preserve the relationship, but also how to slightly jab the listener to encourage a more animated debate. In many Latin-influenced Mediterranean countries, as well as countries in Latin America, animated discussions involve a meeting of the minds. It is advisable to remember this as an invitation for a debate, not a dispute. No solutions are necessary, only the pleasure of exchanging what's on everyone's mind. Americans, who are often desirous of finding a solution to the slightest problem, have the innate need to put an end to any moaning or groaning about complicated issues.

I admit my own tendency to jump in with constructive suggestions, which has often been received as dampening the enjoyment of the heated debate while most everyone else was interested in enlarging the conversation—not putting an end to it. This American KISS style—keep it short and simple—has its advantages in conciseness but can lack the personal touch. Hence, the trend of "If you don't have anything nice to say, don't say anything at all" may have been the precursor for political correctness.

Political Correctness

Even though the origins of political correctness are found in the understandable desire to be more inclusive—not to offend others by being too direct, as well as being conscious of diversity and sensitivity when it comes to the use of some gender offensive words—it has also added more complexity to already-complicated communication patterns. In some instances, it has truly become an impediment to the need for clarity in today's globally dispersed, culturally sensitive workplace. This is because the need for accurate descriptions to avoid the exclusion of certain groups, or labeling people with any specific handicaps, has native English speakers being overly cautious and foreigners receiving frozen stares as they mistakenly refer to the chairman, mailman, or fireman. The subtleties of expressions such as "an opportunity for growth" carefully avoid words like "weakness" or "need for improvement," while an "undesirable consequence" may very well mean that you have been fired.

Being politically correct has yet to be universally exported to non-English-speaking countries. Whenever mentioned, it provokes cynical remarks, which may have to do with its ironic origins along with being misperceived by foreigners as having a connotation of sexual harassment.

A participant in a merger integration workshop in California recounted the story of a highly valued engineer who happened to be part of a carpool with a female colleague. One morning, as the woman was driving up to the company's front entrance, they drove past a female colleague on a bike. Seeing the colleague struggling as she pedaled, the male engineer made a side comment, "She will have to pedal a little faster if she wants to lose the extra pounds she put on this winter." This became the one comment too many, which, shortly afterward, found the highly qualified engineer looking for a new job after being accused of sexual harassment and of not being politically correct in his choice of words— something that to this extent rarely happens outside the United States. As much as I am not condoning verbal slights of this nature, I can only tell you that jibing comments in many countries are meant to be humorous and are still a part of communication patterns in many cultures.

Recently, during a mentor–mentee meeting in a global organization, with more than 100 participants from eight nationalities, a Spanish woman introducing her mentee exclaimed, "When I first saw him, I could only think what a handsome young man. It is a pity that my daughter is only 14!" Dead silence infiltrated the American and British attendees, while Continental Europeans broke into laughter. With these examples in mind, communication within one's own cultural boundaries can be complicated; and going beyond, it can be downright complex.

Beyond Communication: Foods and Friends

The role of food and meals may very well change your attitude when it comes to building relationships. If you think there is a physical or physiological link between opening your mouth and opening your ears, heart, and mind, you may be right. Your brain, not just your stomach, gets hungry. If you skipped breakfast and instead dashed out to that early morning meeting, you most likely increased your edginess as the day started. All of a sudden, that normal rush-hour traffic overwhelms you and makes you mad. A lack of caffeine is blamed for that foggy, not-quite-awake feeling. It has been referred to as low blood sugar, but research is now showing that eating certain food regulates our moods. Foods like oats, bananas, and yogurt produce serotonin—the versatile neurotransmitter responsible for emotional balance and good moods. Surprisingly enough, these are the common ingredients of a well-balanced breakfast (Horstman 2009).

In addition to mood-enhancing capabilities, some foods are more conducive to conversation than others. In the book *Proust was a Neuroscientist*, Jonah Lehrer (2007) explains that back in the early 1900s, the famous French chef Escoffier was known for his renowned veal stock, which is still used today as a basic ingredient in most recipes. Around the same time, a Japanese chemist was discovering a taste known in Japanese as *umami*. From veal stock to soy sauce, a savor had been identified that was later linked to the amino acid glutamate, which is also a neurotransmitter known for its ability to excite people when produced in the brain, along with that of dopamine.

Our bodies only produce about 40 grams of glutamate a day and crave more. When the protein glutamate is broken down through slow cooking, fermentation, or sun-ripening, the amino acid L-glutamate is produced. Foods with the highest concentration of glutamate include aged or cultured cheese, especially Parmesan, tomatoes, and soy. Here's some food for thought: How is it that in cultures known as being more relationship oriented, the national culinary staples contain high amounts of glutamate? Perhaps there is more to the simple serving of monosodium glutamate in Asian cuisine, the pungent odor of aged French cheese, and the sweet savor of sun-ripened tomato sauce combined with parmesan cheese?

What might be going on physiologically when you sit down to share a meal with that friend or colleague? By reducing your unconscious craving for glutamate, you may very well build relationships more easily. Feeling slightly irritable? Perhaps absorbing the serotonin found in oatmeal and yogurt will enhance your mood and facilitate the building of relationships. And whether it is physiological or not, the time invested in developing a rapport is essential, especially when you find yourself in foreign or unfamiliar environments.

Craving comfort food is a common episode in an expatriate's life. Enjoying a good meal is appreciated in every culture—whether the long lunches in many European cultures, the late-night dinners in Latin cultures, or the annual Thanksgiving dinner in the United States. We all come together in search of our need to socially interact and perhaps to replenish our supply of glutamate, which may very well be the glue of relationship building. Eating alone is almost unheard of in some countries. Many a frequent traveler will call room service before stepping into the hotel restaurant and asking for a table for one. Isolation provokes a stressful reaction. Coping with stress often requires assistance or mutual support—the essence of relationships. For more on the importance of meals and food, see the sidebar.

Food as the Foundation for Relationships

When moving to a new place, people often advise us to make new friends to feel more at home. This is great advice, but how can you do it? When it comes to building relationships, we may find some truth to the old wives tale: "To get to a man's (or woman's) heart, go through his (or her) stomach." Relationships are built by spending time together, usually over a cup of coffee, a lunch, or a special dinner. A shared meal leads to sharing ideas and information. While enjoying the most primitive need of survival—nourishment—you let your guard down and become more accepting of others.

As you look for ways to break down cultural and linguistic barriers, you can pick up crucial cultural cues by watching how people share meals—the food they make, the recipes they use, the time it takes to prepare a meal. Is this an on-the-go sandwich society or a crock pot, slow-cooker culture? Meals marinated for hours on end are often a sign of patience for perfection. Deli meat on slices of bread tends to indicate quick building, impatient-to-produce societies. Whatever the attitude and social behavior toward food, enjoying a meal together is often one of the best ways to connect with others and build the foundation for relationships.

Once the food is served, subtle cultural protocols take over. Actively listening to mealtime conversations and observing the learned behaviors of culinary and social rituals provide clues that can help you more effectively interact and start to build a foundation for future relationships. For example, if your colleague expresses appreciation about the freshness of the vegetables being served while comparing them with what he or she recently ate elsewhere, this may imply a true quest for the highest quality and the importance his or her culture places on having or being the very best. Might it also be a possible cue to an underlying belief in perfectionism? Don't be surprised if the extra time spent on a project is devoted to the perfect outcome as a priority, not the deadline.

Building Dynamic Cross-Cultural Teams

How can you build dynamic cross-cultural teams? Let's consider:

- the key ingredients for effective teams
- the details of the seven ingredients of success
- the stages in developing teams
- building and maintaining trust within teams
- learning to care and not compete
- the emotional advantages of team cooperation.

The Key Ingredients for Effective Teams

People come together in work groups or teams to produce what they cannot create individually. The very role of being part of a team is to share the energy and the emotions that empower and engage us. At the same time, it takes a certain mindset to overcome and integrate the unforeseen challenges of aligning local and geodispersed teams, leading multicultural team projects across geographical borders and time zones, and negotiating alliances and partnerships around the globe. To succeed, you need to start building relationships with your colleagues slowly by stepping back and observing how they interact, by looking at the big picture.

Using your observational skills enables you to be attuned to the team's environment. After discovering the team's preferred functioning mode, you can then analyze the details of what should or should not be changed to increase successful collaboration. You can look for visible clues as to how they collaborate as well as visceral cues, which are intuitive. By scrutinizing how others see, feel, and respond to their world, you can then analyze the processes and integrate the bits and pieces that you are intuitively, viscerally, and visually recording in your mind's eye. Following this advice asks you to rely on using the right side of your brain—known primarily as the emotional, intuitive, and creative center. This contradicts everything that you've been taught—that managers are rational and objective (left brain), not emotional and subjective (right brain). That's why working across cultural and linguistic barriers can shock you into seeing things differently.

Intercultural experience enables you to be more aware of how you naturally integrate the use of both brain hemispheres. By learning to empathize with others on their ground, not yours, you become an effective team player. Building relationships on accepting differences—not assimilating, overriding, or ignoring them—is essential so that you can look beyond what differs to what adds value.

Teams are a curious combination of unique people with expectations, perspectives, and the need to develop trusting relationships. As if the dynamics of a traditional team weren't complex enough, today's cross-continent and cross-cultural teams have evolved immensely. Most team members are no longer down the corridor or across from your cubicle, so your recipe for success necessarily includes the spices influenced by your cultural background—made up of primal responses to right and wrong perspectives of how to do something, along with personal and professional experience. You address the dynamics in a multicultural team by identifying each team player's strengths and understanding, not changing how each individual on the team prefers to function and communicate. When this is accomplished, the results are trusting relationships, team coherence, collaborative working environments, and prosperous organizations.

Miscommunication, of course, even occurs in teams where every member is from the same culture, speaks the same language, and sits in the same conference room. Nothing will or ever has been easy when it comes to energizing, empowering, and engaging others. When you add different languages, time zones, and geographical distances, imagine how much we are in dire need of an international recipe for success. Today's international teams vary in sizes and shapes from skip-level (for example, engineers and technicians), to cross-functional (sales and marketing), to project, to self-directed or *kaizen* (quality) work teams, and most all of them are intercultural. They meet regularly, but not often face to face. Unavoidably, underlying issues surge to the forefront when communication styles, interpersonal styles, technological preferences, and culture meet online.

These considerations add more complexity to your international recipe for success. This is today's reality. What has made it more complicated is recognizing the effects of culture. Now that you have developed self-awareness and learned some keys to respectful communication, and steps for building relationships, you can accept that each and every one of us comes with our differences. This coming together of our differences is what makes us a truly effective team—people with different, yet complementary, skill sets, different levels of experience, and layers of interpersonal and cultural differences. The team structure utilizes cooperation to reach objectives and competition to achieve incentives. In search of meeting—and preferably exceeding—objectives, the need to maintain and mobilize individual and collective energy is called encouraging the passion.

With success as the desired outcome, what are the key ingredients of cross-cultural teams? A successful team needs to be made up of individuals who

- can clearly question himself or herself while being comfortable learning from others

- consider himself or herself as professional students of life—willing to learn, innovate, and imagine

- can manage ambiguous situations with the balanced desire to clarify ambiguous communication

- show compassion toward others, clarity, and integrity—consistently walking the talk

- are all-inclusive in their approach, so that all the members' perspectives are taken into consideration and participation is equally distributed

- make sure that every team player has the opportunity to actively take the lead in a discussion or decision-making process

- consistently check that policies and procedures effectively ensure mutual respect.

Details of the Seven Ingredients of Success

Now let's consider the details of the seven ingredients of success. The first ingredient is being able to question acquired knowledge and status.

This establishes a language of trust. The second ingredient encourages calculated risk taking and removes the stigma of failure. And the third ingredient drives the team forward in times of uncertainty while clarifying intentions in case of ambiguity in communication.

The fourth ingredient lays the foundation for consistency and reliability—ensuring the team that you are someone who can be counted on in good times as well as bad. The fifth ingredient removes the complexes that could inhibit the added value that diversity brings to the team and encourages sharing perspectives and leveling language abilities so everyone's voice is heard.

The sixth ingredient establishes well-delegated roles that are interchangeable and participatory. And the seventh ingredient is the glue that consolidates the four-R response mechanism—respect—always mutual, never unidirectional.

High-performing teams are made up of individuals who are accountable to themselves and responsible toward others; their efforts are never self-centered and always made with the goal of building sustainable relationships based on recognizing the need for mutual support and rewards when a well-consolidated team successfully collaborates across cultural and linguistic boundaries.

The Stages in Developing Teams

To succeed in accomplishing the steps outlined above, the dynamics of multicultural teams will necessarily go through the typical phases or stages of any team's development. By studying interpersonal or group structures and task-related activity, the renowned American psychologist Bruce Tuckman described a developmental process in an article first published in 1965, "Developmental Sequence in Small Groups." Initially, he observed a four-stage model—forming, storming, norming, and performing—based on observations of people's behaviors when they first meet in various situations (Tuckman 1965). Here, I elaborate on these four stages.

For teams to work interdependently, "forming" is the foundational, first stage. Essential to this phase is drafting a team charter that defines tasks and identifies rules. Its format includes a clearly articulated mission answering the question of why are we together and recognizes that team members are functionally interdependent, each with a set of strengths so that only by working collaboratively can they accomplish the mission set out before them.

The shared vision of why the team is together is based on corporate and peer-identified shared values. This is the first step in aligning a multicultural team.

The team's charter also should answer questions like "How will we address failed attempts?" "How will we address successful wins?" "And in the end, how will we celebrate?" The process of accepting the cultural variances known as uncertainty avoidance—do you need to have 100 percent perfect results, or are you willing to celebrate a 80/20 or even 60/40 outcome—needs to be part of these early conversations when drawing up the team charter and defining nonnegotiable behaviors for dealing with emotions and ambiguity.

The second step is for the team members to define who their clients are, and what the team's expected outcomes and contributions to your organization are. All this is based on the team's functional objectives, which now need to be developed cooperatively by the members. Letting everyone know that cultural issues are a reality, and, if left out of the conversation or out of the team charter, they will come back to haunt the team's success. At this stage, the team has high hopes and high morale, but low-to-moderate effectiveness as the structure is being formed. A more directive leadership style is a necessary element for the team's development at this initial stage. Miscomprehension of this leadership style as being a sign of authoritative or hierarchal leadership has led some people to believe that this tends toward a cultural norm. Understanding this foundational phase of team development puts the emphasis not on a cultural difference but on effective team dynamics.

The second stage of team development is "storming," as team members negotiate and design strategies. Power struggles often lead to emotions of dissatisfaction, and negative energy is expressed. This can be perceived as conflict, but if constructive, it is the much-needed foundation of integrating interpersonal and intercultural differences. Certain cultural and personal preferences have many team players shying away from this expressive mode of communication, which is necessary for effective collaboration. Some barge ahead, wanting the team to just get down to business, while others are in need of more personal, relational activities.

This is a stage of team development that cannot be avoided but can be productive even if minimized. To ensure the passage of this phase in team development, the role of the team leader is that of a coach who is alert to any in-group/out-group divisions. Cliques, factions, and power struggles are not only detrimental to the team but also produce contagious, irrepressible negative emotions of social exclusion and disengagement. The team leader instills formal and informal mechanisms for giving and soliciting feedback, demonstrates mutual support, and is focused both psychologically and physically on the task.

He or she must have the ability to deal with conflict in a mutually satisfying and positive manner. Acknowledging the impact of cross-cultural values and norms on the team reestablishes the values-added concept of diversity. Such cultural dimensions—known as collective, group, or communitarian orientation—need to be redefined, as well as the models of subjective-versus-objective management styles. The assumption that cultures who are more group oriented will work better together is often misunderstood. If anything, it may very well be the opposite outcome if the team charter does not effectively address reconciling such cultural influences. Relationships remain a driving force in most interactions—whether interpersonal or transactional.

Accepting that people may not put the team's outcome or objectives ahead of its need to establish a good rapport is the key to finding the balance between task and relationship orientations. As seen with the time it takes to develop relationships, the efforts to achieve effective communication requires you to engage emotions during this phase of team development. When the team enters the storming stage, it successfully passes through this emotional phase because the recipe for success is clearly defined in the team charter.

The third stage, norming or bonding, is when team members produce the glue of team coherence called trust. Credibility, accountability, and reliability are some of the ingredients, as well as inclusion. The feeling of belonging, being a part of a group, releases endorphins, those feel-good neurotransmitters. At this stage, information flows freely and cooperation is easily encouraged. The morale is higher as mutual assistance and pride are reinforced. The role of the team leader is that of a facilitator and enabler—calling on individual and team strengths while being alert to potential saboteurs. The team leader encourages effective problem-solving and decision-making processes while celebrating the small wins that will lead to high performance.

With this foundation of the first three stages in place, the team easily moves to the fourth stage, performing, with collaborative competition driving the force that brings them together. By accepting these developmental stages, the multicultural team is enabled to evolve, change, and adapt to the project and the people involved.

To achieve a successful outcome, the team's members need to address intercultural factors from the outset—how they integrate rules, regulations, policies, and procedures with a focus on maintaining healthy relationships. They are committed to a common goal while accepting the uncommon factors that tie them together. Positive aspects of multicultural teams include

- diversity
- multiple perspectives and interpretations
- an openness to new ideas
- more creativity
- higher flexibility
- potentially stronger problem-solving skills
- more extensive culture-specific knowledge, which adds value to the diversity.

Until teams develop trusting relationships and have their individual strengths and contributions recognized, they will stagnate in the first and second stages. They will feel confused, frustrated, and dissatisfied until all the four-R cultural principles are integrated. When the competitive energy resolves itself, performance peaks through stable relations and clear expectations.

Skipping any of the four stages of a multicultural team's development and focusing only on the task and not on the team or lingering too long on building rapport would be detrimental to the team's progress. For instance, not admitting that the team needs to pass through the necessary stage of storming would only leave unresolved issues and suppressed emotions hovering in the background. The return of the repressed emotions could very well erupt in the final stages, minimizing milestone celebrations and leaving team players with feelings of frustration, superficiality, or superiority—all of which will turn the lessons learned process into the blame game.

In 1977, Tuckman, together with Jensen, added a fifth stage, adjourning, to his team development model. This is when team recognition and the individual and collective rewards are important to successfully completing the developmental process. An important element to integrate into this phase is the lessons-learned approach, which is giving positive feedback on what worked, what did not, and what needs to be done differently next time. Structuring this process for best results is essential in not just looking at the past but also especially in transforming the lessons into new actions for future implementation.

Building and Maintaining Trust within Teams

Mutual trust is crucial for any effective team. The winners in today's global teams are those who care about and trust the people with whom they work. If the cultural preferences concerned with energizing, empowering, and engaging teams around the globe are not discussed, trust will diminish. And decreasing trust will lead to disengagement. Research indicates that there are clear links between trust and overall team effectiveness, levels of innovation and creativity, and a team's readiness to adapt and accept change. Establishing an atmosphere of mutual trust is a key challenge for international teams.

A recent survey in *Harvard Business Review* (January 2010) reveals that trust in the workplace has dropped significantly. The numbers break down thus: Among U.S. senior managers, trust is down by 76 percent; among non-U.S. senior managers, down by 51 percent; among academics, down by 21 percent; among customers, down by 18 percent, and among colleagues, down by 10 percent.

How can the members of dynamic multicultural teams counter this depressing situation and instead build and keep trust among themselves? The International Team Trust Indicator (www.worldwork.biz) is an effective tool for identifying the level of trust in a team and how people from other cultures give different emphasis to a range of trustworthiness signals. On the basis of certain trust criteria, the tool identifies levels of trust and the trust "deficit" within any given team or work group. Multicultural teams learn very quickly that respect is based on participation, and mutual respect relies on commitment to the successful outcome and to the clearly defined business objectives. Carrying one's share of the workload and being fully involved in seeking to meet the team's objectives are essential to reaping the rewards of working together, both physiologically and physically.

This is where accountability comes in. Accountability is a natural occurrence if clear communication and courage are practiced by each and every team member, and even more so by the team leader. Consistency in action develops a desire for accountability—expectations are clear, and uncertainty dissolves. Today's global team players and leaders are showing exactly how to achieve the flexibility, clear communication, and transparency so needed in open plan offices or glass-enclosed meeting rooms. By balancing various styles, energizing others with emotional stability, and engaging the trust, you will effectively work and collaborate across the globe.

Learning to Care and Not Compete

In researching this book, the survey I conducted showed that caring for others wins out over competing by a large margin (figure 3-1). In the survey question about caring for others or competing against others, nearly half the participants (49.5 percent) replied that we should give a helping hand to those weaker than ourselves. Competition is fine in its place, but a fine balance between healthy competition and solid collaboration is needed within the context of teams seeking to work effectively together.

Figure 3-1. Caring for Others or Competing Against Others?

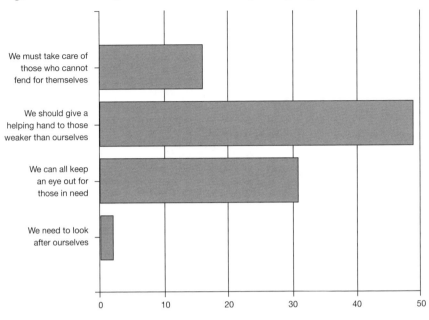

The lesson for team building is clear. After learning to respect people's values, beliefs, and assumptions, and developing the relationships on which we build trust, you can look to eliminate the gaps in mutual understanding to break through the barriers that prevent people from performing at their highest potential. Wherever your travels, teams, leadership experiences, or companies take you, humans will always be human all over the world. Collaborative teamwork, open information, and distributed leadership responsibility will be the source of success for companies in the 21st century.

The Emotional Advantages of Team Cooperation

Our human emotional makeup disposes us to cooperate, and this is a hopeful sign for developing strong teams. We are wired to like, understand, and commit to each other. Neuroscience proves it. For instance,

Marco Iacoboni, a professor and neuroscientist at the University of California, Los Angeles, studies how the "smart" cells in our brains allow us to understand others by demonstrating the existence of mirror neurons. These mirror neurons (discussed in chapter 2 in describing how values and behaviors may develop) engage us to imitate others, and by doing so, we increase our quotient of empathy. Through reliable and consistent behaviors, team members find security through stability, even in ever-changing situations. They know what to expect. These "monkey see / monkey do" neurons connect people through synchronous body movements. The more we use our mirror neurons, the more empathetic we become through unconscious imitation (Iacoboni 2008).

Given these and other recent scientific findings about the human brain and emotions, the time has come to flatten Abraham Maslow's hierarchy of needs—or turn it upside down. Being socially connected is a fundamental need. Earlier in this chapter, the Swiss woman's reaction to her sense of finally belonging, being part of the team, led to an immense feeling of relief and a renewed sense of potential to succeed. Since her arrival, a recurring thought may very well have been "Am I with the right people at the right time?" When you are an employee, working in a team, or leading others, you rely on relationships to get things done. Recognizing other people's efforts and contributions are essential to building trust. When people come together, they form in-groups and out-groups. Recent research has revealed that the pain of social rejection may be more than just metaphorical. The feeling of being hurt may very well be as intense as physical pain. Verbally expressing this pain—"I feel lonely" or "He broke my heart"—is referred to as affective labeling. Studies are showing that the feeling of being socially connected increases a person's sense of self-worth (Eisenberger 2009).

Another way of diminishing painful feelings of loneliness or ostracization when a person is in a foreign environment, or away from loved ones, is simply looking at photographs of loved ones. For instance, recent research has shown that simply holding a loved one's hand when the partner was hidden from sight during stress-induced experiences did not reduce the increased blood flow to the brain (Eisenberger 2009). On the second trial, the participants were asked to look at pictures of their loved ones during a stress-induced experiment. The blood flow to the brain decreased in the areas where the reaction to pain had been identified. Thus, family photos at the workplace may very well serve a purpose—reducing the stress from a feeling of separation or isolation, and thus making employees more productive and serene.

To demonstrate the advantages of effective team building for cross-cultural workplace relationships, let's wrap up this section of the chapter with an exercise that will explore how to empower your team members. This exercise is best suited for four or more people.

Get your team together in a meeting or conference room. Instruct them to sit, make themselves comfortable, and close their eyes. Tell them to think of two different words that describe what they like about team-work. Have them focus on their words and keep them in their mind. Now, instruct the team members, one by one, to call out their first word. When you hear the word, reply, with a strongly negative intonation, "No!" Continue until everyone has suggested their first word. Then ask for the second word. This time, answer, with a strongly uplifting intonation, "Yes!" (This is adapted from an exercise presented by Daniel Siegel at the 2009 NeuroLeadership Summit; see Siegel 2009.)

Then debrief the team; ask the team members how they felt when they heard "no" or "yes." Having done this exercise several times, the answers confirm that the brain has two states—a "yes" state and a "no" state. "Yes" turns on the engagement state. Employees are receptive and creative. In the "no" state, or in an organization where negativity reins, employees don't want to come to work. They do not feel safety or trust. Authority creates a physiological fear state. The brain registers threat, produces disengagement, and increases a loss of focus (Subramanian, Venkateswaran, and Fu 2010).

Now ask your team members if these are characteristics of your workplace environment:

- People want to stay doing the same thing.
- Change is hard.
- Insights are harder.
- Difficult problems seem insurmountable.

- It is hard to stay cool under pressure.

- Others are less inclined to collaborate.

If they answer yes, people are expressing the characteristics of a threat state. An environment based on threat includes not only fear but also all behaviors where avoidance is prevalent—avoid taking risks, initiatives, decisions, speaking up, and contributing (Subramanian, Venkateswaran, and Fu 2010).

Toward Effective Cross-Cultural Coaching

What makes coaching so effective for today's globalized workforce? Working and collaborating around the globe brings new dilemmas to everyday challenges. When facing a dilemma, a person often feels perplexed, uncertain, and incapable of seeing things clearly. To alleviate this stress, companies can, and should, offer workshops where training transfers the needed knowledge to deal with these new challenges and follow-up coaching to accompany employees as they navigate the currents of globalization. Whether you're building teams or seeking to engage employees individually, the cross-cultural workplace really needs a coaching process in place—either with professionally trained external or internal coaches as well as with managers who have learned how to coach. Active listening and powerful questions are the hallmarks of the coaching process and the foundation of relationship building. Here we focus on coaching, as the broader category, so you can see how it fits into the four Rs.

Coaching is a way of making your thinking visible. It is a series of conversations with a purpose. Professionally trained coaches enable clients to reflect on and delve into their deeper potential. Why is it a good tool for sustainable change initiatives?

The Basics of Coaching

If you ask any person going through change "What is the most useful thing a company or friend could provide?" the most common response would be "Someone to call on to help me through this phase." This response is proof that the theory behind coaching works; if someone can talk to another person who will actively listen and ask probing, powerful questions, while focusing on that person's needs and goals, these conversations can have very positive personal and professional effects. Change is difficult because it requires us to question habits and routines—what we take for granted. Coaching addresses the complexity of the intertwining nature of our values, environments, and experiences—while remaining anchored in the present—in an effort to provide multiple perspectives and self-driven solutions. It is a nonjudgmental, nondirective, and, above all, ethical and confidential process with client-directed and person-directed outcomes.

With respect to the four-R formula, coaching combines respect (attentive listening) with relationships (a supportive and reflective dialogue). The coaching process allows clients to apply their realizations to their environments and then to come back, discuss, and assess—What else? What if? Why not? This process is what makes coaching so useful during a change process. This also explains why standard one-time training sessions do not carry participants to sustainable success. Training plus follow-up coaching adds the value of preventing backsliding. As humans and organizations, we exist in the real world and are open, dynamic systems—interactions allow us to grow and evolve. Taking knowledge, applying it, reassessing it, and getting feedback from others and other systems are what we're all about. Just as with the reasoning behind change processes, coaching is a journey toward continuous improvement. Effective coaching is measured by what happens after the session more than by what happens within the session.

Coaching Within the Four-R Context

To explore how coaching can best be done in the context of the four-R formula, let's consider the story of Maria. A drop in profits, a rise in global competition, increased investments in extended product lines, and emerging markets had forced an international Italian fashion design firm to adopt a change management process. It hired Maria, a global executive from the luxury industry, who was raised in Spain, studied in the United States, worked in three countries, and spoke perfect English, along with some Italian. This firm, with its artistic heritage and flamboyant expense accounts, functioned with an indirect communication style, ambiguous objectives, and subjective management.

Maria's team, many of them with 10 to 20 years of experience in this formerly family-run enterprise, were far from welcoming when she arrived on her first day. The change had not been explicitly announced, and her arrival was somewhat of a surprise for those who were not part of the leadership in-group. She did not need a climate survey to detect the cold shoulders, contagious emotional eruptions from some, and unapologetic apathy from others. The workers were stressed. Production almost came to a halt as impatience and incertitude took hold. This was beyond culture, beyond communication. With so much going on behind the scenes, how could Maria even begin to get acceptance for the change management process? She chose to put into action the four universal principles of respect, relationships, recognition, and rewards.

After having identified what needed to change to integrate the challenges and opportunities of globalization, Maria *reviewed* how people were reacting by being attentive to verbal and nonverbal communication, she led them to *regulate* their reactions and emotions by listening attentively to them and making them feel that they were being listened to. In the third action phase of the first universal principle—respect—Maria *evaluated* which behaviors needed to change, and how adaptive she and her team could be while still remaining true to their values. Authentic adaptation produces physical and physiological alignment—the true meaning of authenticity. Being attentive gets the actors' and observers' attention. Ways of showing respect include taking the time to listen to people's concerns, and spending valuable one-to-one face time outside the meeting room, and around the coffee machine, photocopier, or lunch table. To get them actively involved requires a lot more than just poking holes in the panels, as workers do in construction sites. If you want more than just side comments and complaints, ask yourself what happens when you get people's attention: What do they do? They start talking, perhaps even moaning and groaning. And who do they do it with? The people they like, admire, work, and eventually live with. This is the second universal principle—relationships. Change initiatives need to tap into those relationships—the social networking and bonds that bind people together. For cultures labeled as more relationship oriented, and group or interdependent oriented, these networks will be more active, just perhaps not as obvious.

Above, we looked at socialization norms and communication patterns across cultures. We built on our knowledge about implicit and explicit communication styles where verbal and nonverbal behaviors are easily misinterpreted. We learned that our observation skills tell us a lot when appropriately interpreted. By being attentive—to what is happening behind the scenes, to the smiling yes-men, to political correctness, and to the level of absenteeism—we can take the temperature of where people stand on a proposed change initiative. Our ultimate goal is to get them to move, not just stand there. We can do that by using the defined action plan from the second universal principle: relationships.

Relationships are defined by collaborative initiative—that combination of responsibility and accountability toward oneself and others. How does this make change happen? When change is imminent, people reach out to others who are dear to them. We move toward people because we are social beings, we turn to our relationships when we seek support and feel destabilized. A collaborative spirit can only exist when there is nothing to fear, trust is shared, and reciprocity exists. Self-initiative becomes second nature if you know what you're projecting and what others expect.

In the case of Maria, she had to understand the relationship networks within the organization. These included both its official and unofficial hierarchal structures. Organizational charts never reveal the in-groups and out-groups. This explains why more time, more patience, and more encouragement are needed when making change happen across cultures. People have to dare to step out from behind the invisible barriers that have shielded them from collaborating more openly. Those with conservative, low risk-taking values will be the late adopters—or even worse, the early blockers. Enthusiastic supporters can take on the role of mentors or coaches. As mentors, they share advice and experience from other (positive) change initiatives. Their supportive role is one of advisers and guides as they lead others through the change. As coaches, they ask questions, provoke reflection on why the change is necessary, and talk about next steps, envisioning a better future.

Maria was able to identify who could take on which roles. Now it was time to address the emotional needs of those involved in the change process. The third universal principle—recognition—explored in detail in chapter 4—is the ability to see and perceive worldviews through the eyes of others, acknowledging their perspectives, understanding how they feel without being drawn into their internal emotional conflicts.

Now that the change initiative was under way, Maria needed to make sure that communication was clear and that the right people were on the right side of where the change would end up. Why is respectful and clear communication so important? Each person affected by the change is motivated for different reasons with different perspectives; this is why the vision must be inspiring (people want to go there), compelling (people need to go there), and realistic (people can go there). Commitment includes not only getting people to adhere to the change vision but also allocating the time for people to talk about and adhere to the initiative and dedicating a budget so it is not siphoned off existing resources. Corporate communication, informational media support, training, and coaching are some tools that encourage, inform, and speed up the change process.

Maria knew that accompanying the key players during the change process was essential to make change happen and, at the same time, be able to measure tangible outcomes that she could present to the board of directors. She was hired to make this change happen—her job and the organization's future were at stake. She could communicate as much as she felt necessary, but knowledge backfires if it does not translate into action. Insight without input is energy without combustion. She was convinced that training without follow-up coaching would translate into filed-away action plans and fading "eurekas."

Two years later, the international Italian fashion design firm is now a successful global multinational. Maria implemented a change process that took longer than the board of directors had envisioned, but it was successful. With attentive adaptation, Maria identified the early adopters who were capable of breaking down the in-group/out-group barriers. She discovered their strengths, which produced a sense of collaborative initiative—independent yet team-spirited. When they were recognized for how they could affect the successful outcome—remembering that everyone desires a shot at success—they felt rewarded. In chapter 5, we will explore how rewards, the fourth universal principle, are perceived across cultures. What does it mean to be successful? Is it giving to others, giving back to society, or reaching for the stars—for yourself and your immediate family? You'll learn what it means according to cultural theories and frameworks and tie this to the belief that what brings human beings together across the globe is integrating the four universal principles of respect, relationships, recognition, and rewards.

To wrap up this short consideration of coaching, look at worksheet 3-2 and evaluate how coachable you are.

Worksheet 3-2. How Coachable Are You?

Rate yourself: Circle 1 if your answer is no or not at all, and circle 5 if you are in complete agreement with the statement:

I believe that people can change.	1	2	3	4	5
I understand what coaching is.	1	2	3	4	5
I am open to new methodologies.	1	2	3	4	5
I have a good level of self-awareness—a sense of my strengths and weaknesses.	1	2	3	4	5
I have clear expectations of what I want to get out of my coaching sessions.	1	2	3	4	5
I do not mind being challenged or having my point of view questioned.	1	2	3	4	5
When I commit to something, I always do my best to follow through.	1	2	3	4	5
When I have participated in professional development training sessions, I often felt they were one-time events and lacked follow-up.	1	2	3	4	5
I have a very busy schedule but will be able to make time to commit to bimonthly coaching sessions.	1	2	3	4	5
Total (with a score of 20 points or more, you are a good candidate for coaching):					

Questions for Reflection and What's Next

This chapter has three key points. First, making the time to engage with other people is not only enjoyable, but also a sign of respect toward others. Our brains are hardwired with the desire to share—our feelings, our thoughts, our likes and dislikes. These are the elements that bring us together—the social glue that builds trusting relationships. If we start treating people like people, we can build better relationships and organizations that are better off.

The chapter's second key point is that successful teams are not built overnight. They require growth and trust. Remember the stages of team development—forming, storming, norming, performing, and adjourning. What makes our lives successful and meaningful? The relationships we build on our journey in life. People commit to people because we appreciate others not for who they are but for how they make us feel.

Third, coaching can guide your organization in accomplishing sustainable change, which can only take place when behaviors are aligned and enacted upon in accordance with the change initiative. The coaching process requires people to reflect on ingrained habits, decide what works and what doesn't, learn about processes and tools for improvement, and then apply both knowledge and support to sustain the process. In the context of effective coaching, the processes of accepting, adjusting to, and sustaining change are directly tied to the four universal principles of respect, relationships, recognition, and rewards.

Now consider these questions:

1. With every interaction, we start to build or fail to build a relationship. How well do you build long-lasting, sustainable ones?
2. What actions can you take to expand your comfort zone?
3. How can you assist friends and colleagues in integrating new teams or developing a sense of belonging?
4. What benefits can be reaped—for each of us as individuals, team members, and leaders—from random acts of kindness?
5. What does the word "coaching" conjure up in your mind?

6. What benefits can coaching offer to you, your friends, and your colleagues around the globe?

Chapter 4 explores how recognition is a driving force in all of us—from the modest, low-profile habits of egalitarian and communitarian cultures to the need to be number one in competitive cultures. You'll find out how we can all contribute better to unleashing talent across hallways, continents, and cultures. How can organizations meet the needs of today's global teams so interconnected in ways unheard of in the past? Recognition—essential to producing those feel-good neurotransmitters—is an essential part of the puzzle.

Recognition Across Cultures

Today, many American corporations spend a great deal of money and time trying to increase the originality of their employees, hoping thereby to get a competitive edge in the marketplace. But such programs make no difference unless management also learns to recognize the valuable ideas among the many novel ones, and then finds ways of implementing them.

—Mihaly Csikszentmihalyi

Clues to the meaning of *recognition* in the context of the cross-cultural workplace can be found in this word's etymology. In its basic form, "recognize," it originally meant "resume possession of land," from the Middle French *reconiss-*, from the stem *reconoistre*, "to know again, identify, recognize," from the Old French, from the Latin *recognoscere*, "acknowledge, recall to mind, know again, examine, certify" (thanks again to Douglas Harper's *Online Etymological Dictionary*, www.etymonline.com). The connotations here are telling—the sense of looking back and reclaiming something that was temporarily lost, and now seeing its true value.

The Essential Missing Ingredient

Recognition is the essential missing ingredient to retaining talent. A simple gesture of appreciation is often overlooked. Recognizing how individuals and teams have contributed to adding value to a final outcome brings more to the competitive edge than all the academic research, engagement questionnaires, and team assessments so dear to top managers when asking how their company can be more competitive in today's globalized markets. Recognition is often left by the wayside with a hasty "thank you" or a minor bonus—if not completely overlooked. It still surprises companies when engagement surveys demonstrate low morale or a lack of collaboration. When was the last time you simply recognized a colleague's effort, input, or loyalty? An odd word, loyalty—it might very well be a word that Generations X or Y will find unfamiliar in a globalized landscape, where mobility will be determined by who appreciates whom in the competitive race for talent management.

Given these clues, and now that you have learned quite a bit about how people function when they expect respect—through their values, beliefs, and preferred behaviors—and how team structure and contagious emotions are essential elements of how people interact with others through relationship building, it is time to shift perspectives from *me* to *we*. Up until this point, the book's focus has been on how each of us wants to be treated, and it is now time to look at how others want to be treated. So this chapter asks and seeks to answer these questions:

- What can each of us do to improve upon and to reinforce our relationships around the globe?
- How will clearly recognizing the qualities and needs of the people with whom I work change our global workplace?
- How do organizations find the right people and keep them in the right place at the right time, all the time?

Respect and relationships will get these high-potential executives on board; recognition and rewards will keep them there—particularly in relation to cross-cultural considerations. For one such person's experience, see the sidebar.

> After his first year in Europe, an American global executive explained his experience: "I have learned that culture shock is not about what's different, but what others do differently (and, in many cases, better)! If I hadn't had the opportunity to work with a multicultural, geographically dispersed team, I might never have thought about resolving some of the issues the way we did. It's true that encouraging internal critics and clarifying assumptions of underlying beliefs and different points of view has been exhausting. Those are some of the reasons why it takes more time to work across time zones, languages, and cultures—but it's amazing when it works well! By recognizing each and every person's contribution to a better outcome, we reinforce the richness of diversity. This cross-cultural experience has made me realize that I have been living and thinking in a silo for most of my professional life."

We'll look at rewards in chapter 5, but here let's focus on recognition. Understanding business goals in foreign cultures will give you the quantum leap to hiring the best above the rest, and get them to go the extra mile as challenges and opportunities energize and inspire them.

In chapter 3, the six-step empowerment exercise showed how positive reinforcement releases feel-good neurotransmitters in our brain. This underlines the human need for recognition. Simply put, what we all want in life is a shot at success—the emotional high that gives us the recognition for achieving what, at first, was thought to be unattainable. These achievements wouldn't be possible without the belief others— friends, family, managers, and colleagues—have in us. When people are given the opportunity to achieve recognition, they can be motivated by a number of different things, ranging from personal satisfaction to exceeding defined objectives to pleasing others—colleagues, managers, family members. Whatever the reason, the driving force is the source of motivation.

To help you home in on the dynamics of recognition at the outset, try worksheet 4-1. This exercise is aimed at recognizing behaviors that bother you and redefining them in a positive perspective. As it has often been said in various ways by various scholars, if you see something you don't like, change it. If you can't change it, change the way you look at it.

Worksheet 4-1. Revealing Patterns of Recognition

Find three to five stakeholders among family, friends, or colleagues to do this exercise with you. By getting the conversation going—and making everybody, including yourself, aware of your perception and the admired perception—patterns of change, adaptation, and recognition will be easier to attain, decipher, and sustain.

20/20 Vision	20/20 Vision	20/20 Vision
Time needs to be managed	Open information sharing	
What do you admire most about the opposite value— time is flexible?	*What do you admire most in the opposite behavior (that is, selective sharing of information)?*	
Example:	Example:	
When time is flexible, you can adapt better to a changing environment.	By not openly sharing information, this person has a high appreciation for confidentiality.	
	What do you admire most in this behavior?	What do you admire most in this behavior?

Discuss the opposing views with the person concerned and come up with an acceptable behavior or attitude that incorporates both views. Perhaps being flexible in some circumstances is acceptable, but not in others.	Discuss the opposing views with the person concerned and come up with an acceptable behavior or attitude that incorporates both views. Perhaps being explicit about when and why information is shared or not will avoid recycling unresolved conflicts.

Note: The heading "20/20 Vision" refers to visual acuity—the ability to clearly see something. It means that when you stand 20 feet away from a chart, you can see what the "normal" human being can see. In this exercise, 20/20 vision invites you to step back and ask yourself: What do I value most? Is it, as in the examples, managing time or open information sharing? When you decide what drives you, think about the opposite, or allergic, reaction to what you find admirable. Then focus on the behaviors that at first may irk you, but upon reflection may intrigue you. Ask yourself, as in the examples: What prevents me from seeing the added value of flexible time? What can be the advantages of not openly sharing information? Give examples, and discuss these perceptions and behaviors with family, friends, and colleagues. Getting the conversation going is the best way to break down barriers and shift perspectives.

Motivating People to Pursue Recognition

An individual's success in companies is often measured by how he or she meets or exceeds corporate objectives and expectations. The questions you need to ask are

- What do you identify as the driving factors behind motivation and engagement?
- What does the other person identify as the driving factors behind motivation and engagement?
- How do we each encourage one another's efforts?
- How do we distinguish between motivation and inspiration?
- What inspires us—both individually and across cultures?
- How do we align these driving forces in a sustainable manner?

To maintain the engagement required in today's constantly changing world, we all need to understand that cultural expectations may divide us, but investing in some old-fashioned recognition will unite us. The difficulty in applying something as simple as recognition is finding the right method, the right tools, the right time, and the right place to do so in cross-cultural interactions.

Recognition and Culturally Learned Behaviors

Now let's take a look at the relationship between recognition and culturally learned behaviors. In doing this, first, it's useful to break down the factors in recognition. And then it's important to look at how recognition can be encouraged.

The Factors in Recognition

In a 2008 global recognition study conducted by Towers Perrin for O. C. Tanner, thousands of people in 13 countries were interviewed about appreciation and engagement in the workplace. The study found that appreciation, opportunity, and well-being are the factors that drive engagement across industries, cultures, and the world. When you give or receive encouragement, it rewards the heart. The strong correlation between enhanced company financial performance and augmented global talent management practices strengthens the intuitive belief that business success depends on talented, engaged high performers. People thrive when they are discovered for a specific skill or quality, are nurtured according to their personalities, and are recognized for their efforts.

Let's look at how culture influences recognition during those formative years, well before companies start to recognize people's strengths and talents. In France, as in most of Europe and many countries in Asia, educational systems have been built on hierarchal, and often centralized, government-determined curriculums. Teachers are not, as is often the case in the U.S. system, partners in education but are more gateway controllers deciding who passes through and who doesn't. They are demanding and conservative, preferring negative reinforcement.

In the United States, however, though the environment is still competitive, the reinforcement is quite positive. The teacher's job consists of identifying students' strengths and persuading them to achieve their recognized potential. At parent-teacher meetings in America, teachers most always have some level of praise to share with the parents. Children at a very early age give teacher feedback—some even catapulting teachers into receiving the famed "teacher of the year" awards, with mention in local newspapers. This is something unheard of in many countries, where teachers are considered irreproachable. Many foreign curriculums are geared to enable students to acquire a complete education by rote memory. Asking for or receiving feedback is rare, if not utterly condemned.

A recent attempt in France to publish a list where teachers were ranked by student appreciation over the Internet (www.note2be.com) was considered illegal by the government agency protecting information on the Internet. Blogs have surfaced, but nothing official has been authorized. The general curriculum in France is heavily weighted toward mathematics, and classes are mixed by level, with the assumption that students are considered equal in their ability to receive a broad-based level of cultural instruction in 10 subjects. The ultimate goal is passing the final exam, the baccalaureate, preferably with a science major, because everything else is considered second degree or failure. Early-orientation programs for technical studies, low grades, and negative reinforcement—you are never good enough—can result in a vulnerable person in need of protection. Parent–teacher meetings are most often held to emphasize how even the best student in the class needs to work more, focus better, or improve something. Praise or even simple recognition of work well done is very rare. Given these educational realities, it is thus not surprising to learn that much intercultural research has found many French people (and likewise, other Europeans with similar educational systems) to be risk averse, modest, and lacking in self-initiative.

Neuroscience is proving that negative feelings incite a cerebral process whereby, at worst, cognitive function shuts down or, at best, thought processes are impaired, putting a person in a high-alert state of threat. How does this affect a person in the later years? When a young adult enters the workforce, the lack of having received recognition is hardwired in his or her brain. This may very well explain reactions from Europeans—when asked "When was the last time you thanked a colleague at work?" the answer is often "Why would I? They are doing their job!" Not to make this sound that others outside of the United States are ungrateful, but Europeans typically are uncomfortable with openly praising others. They reply that they are modest and honest—whether the egalitarian Dutch, who tend to seek a consensus and have realistic views, or the Germans, who lean toward hierarchy and expertise. The British remain low key, while the reactions of many of the French are based on recognition being quickly affiliated with acquiring a long-standing status. Taking the risk of praising someone if his or her chances of a repeat performance are in jeopardy seems somehow unfair. Asians, in their educational style of recognizing first the group and not the individual, do not have a preconditioned reflex of putting themselves as individuals in a more advantageous light. In many countries, praise is often perceived as manipulative. Add to that the rhythmic intonation in the American pronunciation, along with superlatives, and the stereotype of Americans being superficial is now reinforced.

Encouraging Recognition

So how can we work and collaborate with all these preexisting conditions of expectations and perceptions? How can we adapt our behaviors while still remaining authentic and not provoking suspicion? Most important, how can we apply this knowledge and understanding to our approach to recognizing others? Once again, we need to get the conversation going. How could an American colleague imagine that what might be perceived as a French colleague's arrogance is really due to a protective shield of vulnerability? Studies have shown that even in the United States, talking about our feelings in public stretches our comfort zones—it requires us to show our emotions.

The idea that these "soft" skills don't belong in our professional arena is really based on the fear that emotions evoke—vulnerability, subjectivity, and favoritism. It also takes time to listen attentively, balance your communications style with advocacy and inquiry, and choose the words that encourage the heart, ignite the passion, and engage the people around you. But the results are higher commitment, engagement, productivity, and team coherence. The time saved in the long run, the people factor multiplied by hundreds, and the reduced turnover make this a formula for success. We now know that, as humans, we all crave recognition.

Determining the dosage, the source, and the reasons behind how to apply recognition can be confusing in cross-cultural interactions. So how can we do these things? One way is to make sure that an attitude of gratitude is part of the team charter or corporate values. Many foreigners will be surprised when they read about this attitude in the policies-and-procedures manuals of corporate governance, but they will be less surprised when employees walk the talk. It is true that choosing the right dose of appreciation is at first a delicate operation. Too much of anything can make people suspicious. Yet recognition when we least expect it, and it's well dosed, is fundamental. Without it, emotional distress accumulates over time, wearing down passion and commitment.

Pursuing Recognition Initiatives in the Cross-Cultural Context

How can you pursue recognition initiatives in the cross-cultural context of the globalized, globally dispersed workplace? First, you must gain an awareness of the relevant cultural variations. And then you need to pursue a logical, orderly process.

Gaining Awareness

If working and collaborating around the globe has you traveling to foreign countries or corporate sites abroad, learning to observe with whom and in which ways others interact is essential to knowing which recognition initiatives to put into place. Carefully observe your surroundings and your colleagues' behaviors, and then ask yourself:

- How do people dress—formally or informally?
- Do people use first names with each other?
- Are people consulted about policies that affect them?
- Does everyone have lunch in the same place?
- Do people socialize out of work?
- Do people make jokes? What makes them laugh?
- Do people keep strict times?
- How are appointments arranged and respected?
- How is information communicated, with whom, and by whom?

These observations are keys to becoming well informed, which includes knowing the local customs as well as office policies and local labor laws. Collecting this information will pave the way for implementing recognition initiatives. Before you are ready to apply your observations to decipher recognition preferences, however, you need to meet with your colleagues face to face. This one-to-one time will help confirm or deny your observations, and from there you can begin to understand what recognition means for these individuals in this environment.

In addition, understanding official and unofficial networks will make the job easier when it comes to getting the conversation going. If your team is geographically dispersed, a local mentor is essential to serve as your key contact in obtaining this information. Even if the team is dispersed around the globe, Internet technology is there to help, not hinder communication. Virtual communication includes emails, conference calls, and shared documents as well as occasions to celebrate milestones, which can be anything from a virtual high-five to recording your teams' very own YouTube concert. Because communicating via email requires low-context, direct transmission of information, respect and relationships become even more important. Recognition is done using this very same technology—after checking policies concerning who to copy on the email and who not to copy. Setting up an intranet team space with a wall for photos allows for people to share openly and privately—a great way of reinforcing the respect, bonding those relationships, and recognizing the need that co-workers want to have ongoing communication and increased information flow with their colleagues around the world. Just look at the popularity of blogs, social networking media, and other digital networks.

Pursuing the Process

Once the structure is in place, rotating delegated roles will ensure that people don't get bored by a standardization or burned out by an obligation and keep their sense of recognition fresh. To enable you to do this, follow a three-step process. First, connect with co-workers on a one-to-one basis. Use techniques like a wall of profile and personal photos or a schedule for celebrations. Communicating both small professional wins and personal milestones among those people who want to share such information will motivate and increase the ties to a sense of organizational belonging.

Second, seek to understand the organization, including its goals and vision and its global dimensions. Knowing who is who, and tying up the loose ends between what is happening in the Delhi, Hong Kong, and San Diego offices, will build support and bring the significance of the big picture vision into a more local focus.

And third, identify those celebrations that have more meaning for local teams and individuals. A local tradition—including, and beyond, events like end-of-year celebrations or even the personal milestones that some people may not feel comfortable sharing—can be an excuse for celebrating in a more global sense.

Examples of these kinds of local traditions that can be celebrated— or at least appreciated—by your global team include the Polish tradition of celebrating the feast days of the saints for whom people are named—so Saint Marie's Day is the anniversary celebration for everyone named Marie, Mary, or Martin—and the French tradition that celebrates the patron saints of industries—such as the celebration of Saint Eloi's Day by those in the plumbing industry. And then there are national saints' days and major religious feasts—such as the Irish celebration of Saint Patrick's Day and Muslims' Eid ul-Fitr, often abbreviated to Eid, the three-day holiday marking the end of Ramadan. Making these celebrations recognized events for individuals or the national team without feeling the need to be politically correct due to a lack of inclusion of the entire team opens curiosity and discussion about local customs, beliefs, and motivations.

Recognizing Strengths, Competencies, and Talent

Where do strengths come from? How do we encourage strengths in others? What are the differences between strengths, competencies, and talent? Answering these questions is the key to understanding how to recognize the efforts committed employees invest in themselves, in their teams, and in the organization. Keeping good employees energized, empowered, and engaged means discovering and developing their strengths, competencies, and talents. But what are the differences among these three things, and why does it matter?

Let's start with talent. This pertains to naturally occurring, preferred activities at which individuals (employees) succeed without much effort; they will gravitate toward these kinds of activities that use their innate abilities. Competencies can be defined as learned abilities, well-defined behaviors, and capabilities that allow an employee to successfully perform the tasks required on the job or in the workplace. Strengths are enhanced talents combined with competencies and the added component of proper application. These may or may not be used in the workplace, especially if left unidentified. We build upon our talents—creating strengths—for a more meaningful purpose in life, both personally and professionally.

Identifying employees' innate talents, building these into strengths, and enabling them to acquire the necessary competencies affects performance because it makes employees feel good about themselves, increasing their status and reinforcing relationships. According to David Rock's brain-based model for collaborating with and influencing others—SCARF, meaning status, certainty, autonomy, relatedness, and fairness (Rock 2008)—both intrinsic and extrinsic motivators increase when status rises, uncertainty decreases, autonomy is high, relationships are solid, and fairness is exemplary. Think back to that person who made you feel good about yourself (increasing status) and believed in you (increasing autonomy). More than likely, this person was explicit in what he or she expected of you (decreased uncertainty), was someone with whom you had a good relationship (relatedness), and was someone who treated you fairly. How did this make you feel? Capable, strong, and empowered—right? Our human nature is to seek rewards and avoid threat (Gordon 2009).

So, when your talents are discovered by someone else and you are encouraged to use them, the feelings of recognition—appreciation, belonging, and a sense of being important—are motivating. Through clarity in communication—an important ingredient in working and collaborating around the globe—you establish the give–give rapport. The motivation is in knowing that if you put in the effort, it will be recognized. These strengths come from knowing your values, which you translate into your behaviors. When they are recognized by co-workers, managers, or leaders, they reinforce your deepest core drivers and you become more engaged.

The question of how to recognize particularly exemplary behavior can only be answered in the context of a particular organization. So instead of abstract or simplistic answers, consider the suggestive sidebar about Charlie and Wolfgang.

Global organizations are changing with the times. Taking what works well elsewhere, promoting what comes from home, and mixing these together to get the right recognition prescription is essential—that is what it means to effectively collaborate across the globe. Wherever you are, people want recognition and, even though hesitant at first, are usually willing to give it a try. When it doesn't fit their value systems, they leave. The basis for the Charlie and Wolfgang sidebar was that

Charlie and Wolfgang: Harmonizing the Communication of Objectives and the Celebration of Milestones

The importance of getting the recognition prescription right is illustrated in this story about a situation in which communicating objectives and celebrating milestones had become contradictions. Charlie, the firm's global retail director, who had recently arrived in Paris from Los Angeles, listened attentively to his German colleague, Wolfgang, the European sales director, as he explained that his primary concern with the European sales team was a lack of ownership when it came to sales targets.

Wolfgang gave a thorough explanation of how he met with each country and regional sales manager individually to discuss their annual sales targets. He was always open and available to share his expertise during the year, but he maintained a more hands-off leadership style. He believed that the managers in place were serious, committed, and capable of running their markets. Stretch targets, tightly timed meeting agendas, and professional respect were characteristics of his professional style. Wolfgang assured Charlie that the slump in sales was just a passage the European team needed to get through; times were tough, and markets were competitive.

Charlie had been sent to France for a two-year assignment from the firm's Global Headquarters to its European Headquarters to get international experience and to find out what could be done to help his European counterparts better meet sales goals. As he listened attentively to his German colleague explain his managerial processes, he couldn't help thinking, "We're an IT company: young, innovative, and profitable. What's going on here?"

Following up on Wolfgang's perception about a lack of team spirit, Charlie decided to inject some enthusiasm into the next sales meeting scheduled via a conference call in a week's time. Right after Wolfgang introduced Charlie, he jumped in, telling personal anecdotes about the challenges of his new life in Paris. He then focused his questions on getting to know everyone, personally. His communication style was direct and open—listen first, talk later. When he asked everybody to talk about their most recent successes, he was friendly and supportive, focusing more on the personal and the positive rather than on the challenges and the professional.

During the sales meeting in June, Charlie arrived laid back, polite, and respectful of others but genuine in his approach. By this time, people felt they knew him. He certainly knew them. He seemed to remember every success story shared—whether personal or professional. He remembered who had kids and whose family member had a skiing accident or another who had recently become a grandfather. He shook hands coming and going, slapped the occasional shoulder, and genuinely showed he cared for everyone in that room.

After the meeting, Charlie put into place a new policy nobody had imagined would be possible. He announced that there would be a change in procedures for sales forecasting. Instead of the individual meetings where targets were discussed, they would now be announced openly via the monthly conference calls with everybody attending from around the world—an effort to add accountability to the new team spirit. Calls were set up on rotating time zones, with the request that whenever there was someone all alone in a remote location, everyone else would also remain in their office, alone, to call in for the conference.

This put everybody on the same leveled playing field. There would be no comical side remarks in a jovial conference room for some while others were participating alone. After each country's sales targets were recorded on the first call, the monthly follow-up call included mini win–win celebrations and sincere recognition for meeting milestones and exceeding expectations.

People were amazed that Charlie's approach worked. Was there overall acceptance? No. Did he make some enemies and lose some status? Yes. But by the time the country managers knew he meant business—that he walked the talk and they could rely on him being there, supporting them, empathizing with them, and cheering them on as they faced their challenges and setbacks—Charlie's style had become part of the company DNA—determined and necessary achievements.

In the past, the firm's organizational culture had been characterized by indirect communication styles, with argumentative conversations around coffee machines. Coolness, calmness, and conflict avoidance had been key components at meetings, along with a generally hierarchical approach and subjective management style. The outcome had been many apathetic people who didn't care and were not cared for. What did Charlie do? He showed them where he stood, what he cared for—the business outcomes and who he cared about—all of them. In the end, what else really counts? Finally, how did Charlie know to take these effective actions? What do you think? This sidebar is meant to be suggestive, to provoke your thinking. For instance, how were Charlie's actions informed and shaped by his growing cultural awareness—as a Californian and American—of the need to give ongoing, genuine recognition to his colleagues?

Charlie shared with me those first three, very difficult months when he was in the midst of the storm. Everyone seemed to be telling him he just couldn't do it his way. But he did. He took the risk with the promise that it would be a give–give, win–win collaboration. He didn't refer to the corporate values, he lived them—direct communication, energize others, collaborative teamwork, drive performance—all these values had behaviors he portrayed, everyday.

Charlie admits that at times, he was certainly considered the "ugly American," but he recently heard some French suppliers discussing what he had done. One was saying how it was unimaginable to do something like that in their company, while the colleague said, "Maybe we should try it—that'll shake up the hierarchy and perhaps the business results for the better!"

Can foreigners adopt foreign behaviors? Charlie couldn't become more formal, hierarchal, and authoritative. Those weren't his values, and they weren't the company's values. What did he do? He remained authentic, open, and willing to share his intentions and expectations, to seek compromise, promote cooperation, and develop collaboration, and especially to communicate not only what he cared about—the company—but also whom he cared about—the team.

Can clarity, transparency, and honesty in communication be part of employee expectations around the globe? Look back at the number one value chosen by the survey participants—honesty (figure 2-1 in chapter 2). Ambiguity, subjectivity, and implicit, high-context communication may still be the case within some monocultural groups, but today, not one country in the world is monocultural. When employees understand how their specific job contributes to achieving success across the board—for them as individuals, other team members, and the business objectives—they become more committed to the overall outcome. People like to know how success will be measured and how they can best be a part of that success.

Research has shown that when objectives are ambiguous and the "fit" between the company's expectations (as identified by the employee's competencies and strengths) are not aligned, then the outcome is disengagement. This translates into a decrease in productivity and/or the loss of the employee. The unrecognized, talented executive who becomes disengaged will eventually be recognized—often by a competitor. Companies are then found hurrying to replace executives and get newly hired staff members up to speed within a short time frame. Even in the midst of an economic downturn, the global talent race is on.

Today's climate dictates that you understand how to develop employees' competencies, strengths, and talents to align with the company's needs, and then recognize and reward them. Yet the best person to ask about strengths is the person using them. How do you recognize your strengths? Aside from assessment tools—like Gallup's StrengthsFinder 2.0, devised by Tom Rath (see http://www.strengthsfinder.com/113647 /Homepage.aspx)—you are the only person who can determine what you like about your job.

Understanding at which moment during the day you find yourself so focused—a sensation of "flow"—that you don't see the time fly is a good indicator that you are using your innate talent. When you discover this moment, look for a job or the opportunity to utilize this aspect of who you are. This is how you develop strengths—much like a muscle, you develop your talents by using them. Not only is it easy to do something you like doing; in turn, you develop resilience. It is easy to work under stress if what you are doing is what you enjoy doing. So, as Benjamin Franklin is quoted as saying, "Hide not your talents. They for use were made. What's a sundial in the shade?"

Eliminating "Us" versus "Them"

If you take research from the field of psychology and apply it to the last 30 years of intercultural research, you will see similarities. Like the psychologists who initially focused on improving weaknesses instead of developing talents, intercultural scholars sought to focus on differences based on the hypotheses that similarities prevented us from recognizing our differences. This early intercultural research promotes the "us/them" frame of mind that then risks being reinforced when individuals are exposed to the slightest differences between cultures. Today, by underlining what divides us, we tend to build more barriers instead of bridges.

Positive psychology must be applied to cross-cultural scholarship. Instead of an "us–them" mindset, it needs to focus on having a "me–we" mindset. This frame of mind is about knowing what makes each of us unique. The "me" is knowing how your culture influences your behaviors, how those culturally influenced behaviors are perceived by others, and how discovering the strengths within these behaviors allows you to work more collaboratively with colleagues around the world. In a "we" mindset, you focus on the multicultural team to which you belong, the confluence of the group's unique strengths and cultural contexts. It is no longer just about profitability but more about using unique talents to succeed together.

Motivation and Engagement in a Borderless World

Motivation and engagement are both essential to developing and retaining productive employees. It is important to note how these two feelings differ:

- Motivation is short-lived and brain based.
- Engagement is a set of long-lasting feelings developed from emotional commitment.

Tasks or responsibilities motivate. In communicating their organization's vision and inspiring hope in the future, global leaders get what they give. They must be optimistic, future oriented, and energetic. By being authentic, they demonstrate courageous and committed communication. In return, they get followers who are accountable. Global leaders who are energetic, emotionally attuned, and empathetic find themselves surrounded by engaged followers—around the globe.

R R
R R Questions for Reflection and What's Next

Recognition is reaching out to others, respecting them in all their diversity, and showing the empathy so needed in today's world while remaining detached enough to energize, empower, and engage people. We all crave simple recognition for our efforts. This chapter's key points include how we all naturally have the need to be appreciated, and thus recognized. This is best done by shifting our perspective from me to we. When you look to others for encouragement and support, you reinforce your need to belong—to be part of a bigger purpose. Learning to look beyond initial irritations, you focus your attention on what attracts you to others, not on what distracts you. You develop relationships through an attitude of gratitude—the simple recognition of how each of us brings value to the table.

Now consider these questions:

1. How is recognition typically given in your organization?
2. How can reconciling the ways you perceive and recognize others lead to more valuable, respectful, and rewarding relationships?

In chapter 5, by focusing on the fourth universal principle—rewards—you'll learn how the most enriching rewards are not monetary or tangible, they are those that convey meaning and a sense of belonging. The real reward is an understanding that "we" are the world—not individually, but collectively.

Chapter 5

Rewards Across Cultures

The highest reward for a man's toil is not what he gets for it but what he becomes by it.

—John Ruskin

Just as with recognition, clues to the meaning of the word "rewards" can be found in its etymology. It comes from an Old Northern French word meaning "take notice of, watch over, guard," and later came to be related to any form of "requital or repayment for some service" (thanks again to Douglas Harper's *Online Etymological Dictionary*, www.etymonline .com). In the context of the cross-cultural workplace, taking notice of someone or applying compensation and benefits in an equitable manner around the globe leads to a complicated juggling of figures and formulas that has left more than one human resources executive betwixt and between, if not utterly bewildered. What is motivating for some runs the risk of demotivating others. So what is it that we need?

Success and happiness—these are two quests in every life. Our life stories give foundation to our beliefs, perceptions, and expectations. In turn, these influence our quest for success and happiness, from "can-do" convictions to beliefs in fate and destiny. It has been said that success is getting what you want, happiness is wanting what you get. Both are rewards for living a fulfilled life, achieving a purpose, and investing time, energy, and often money in reaching these goals. This brings us to "rewards," the fourth universal principle.

Across cultures, opinions differ as to what designates a reward. Is it the award itself, or the recognition for having achieved something? Does the significance of a reward increase or decrease if it is individually received? What about if it is equally distributed among the members of a team? This chapter seeks to answer these questions and also to discuss these:

- Who designates the worthiness of a reward—the giver or the receiver?

- How can cross-cultural reward scenarios be misinterpreted?

This chapter considers the relevance of cultural frameworks and theories for people trying to implement global business strategies of compensation and motivation. The chapter does not go into depth about the globalization of pay systems or other human resource management processes that are available to global organizations. This book is about people and perspectives, not policies or procedures.

What motivates you more? High gains over a short period of time or meaningful, smaller rewards over the long term? The shape and size of the rewards are based on our individual preferences, our contextual influences, and our culturally learned behaviors—what we value the most, or what others perceive as valuable. And a lack of rewards can be devastating; see the sidebar.

Who designates the worthiness of a reward—the giver or the receiver? Much like beauty being in the eyes of the beholder, the true value of a reward can only lie with the person who receives it. The giver of a reward influences the value of the reward not in what it contains but in how it is presented. And though the reward itself can vary from memorabilia to monetary gain, its significance is in the unexpectedness of receiving it more than in its consistency.

How can cross-cultural reward scenarios be misinterpreted? Companies that use pay-for-performance reward systems—where pay incentives and rewards link employee knowledge, skills, and contributions to organizational results—will motivate employees coming from cultural backgrounds where individualism is valued (primarily the United States,

> A high-level executive in a global corporation recounts the consequences of a lack of rewards: "My passion was the company. Friends and family kept telling me I gave too much—of my time, of my energy, of my love—to the organization. It didn't matter, because somehow I assumed that I'd be rewarded one day. When I heard, after the fact, that they had filled the position I was eyeing, I was devastated. They had immediately looked outside the company, without even letting me know that the position was available. I didn't even have the opportunity to interview for it. I felt they didn't respect me or my efforts. The relationships I had developed over the years meant nothing. They never recognized my commitment. So I lost the passion and left the job. They couldn't believe it when I handed in my resignation."

United Kingdom, and parts of Canada). Studies have shown that this short-term monetary perk is not always beneficial for multicultural teams because the motivational factor is often short-lived.

Intercultural research defined national cultures as either *independent* (individualist) or *interdependent* (group oriented). Each culture motivates and compensates its members in exactly the opposite ways. Just as the word "independence" implies, a culture based on independence or individualism (for example, those of the United States, Canada, and, more recently, some Eastern European countries) is not influenced by the thought or action of others. Its focus is more on individual or single-minded contributions. Conversely, the word "interdependent" underlines both the fact of being mutually dependent and mutually beneficial to one another. Just pick up any newspaper while traveling in Europe to read about the strife over the European Union's regulations as countries squabble about how they regard mutual assistance, social benefits, and equality, among other issues. Neuroscience and the rise of social networking media are proving the contrary. People around the world, not national cultures, are influenced by how others feel. Emotions are contagious—and, of course, jealousy and compassion are human emotions.

Even so, when these issues are part of the global workforce, the clash of cultures becomes unavoidable—with the most extreme contrasts being between the predominant Eastern and Western cultural mindsets. Relationship-oriented cultures, like many of those in the East, tend to lean toward subjective management, where rewards are weighed in how much the giver appreciates the person receiving the reward and not necessarily the job performed. Conversely, task-oriented cultures, like many of those in the West, tend to regard reward compensation as part of the contract—clear objectives lead to a job well done, which in turn is well rewarded. Regarding this type of situation, see the sidebar.

Finding the Right Reward

The task of finding the right reward will be clarified if you follow several logical steps. First, identify the types of rewards that would be appropriate. Second, consider the various factors in offering rewards. And third, apply the four Rs to rewards.

Types of Rewards

There are many kinds of rewards in the globalized workplace—from a framed certificate to gift certificates, from monetary compensation to developmental promotions. Basically, however, these rewards can be broken down into two types: extrinsic and intrinsic.

Extrinsic rewards include increased pay, employment security, promotion, status, relationships, and work conditions. These kinds of rewards

One women I interviewed seemed genuinely bewildered. Her husband, a professor, had just been offered a position at a renowned university in the United States, and he didn't want to accept it. We were having lunch together as she explained: "They are willing to pay for our expatriation, our temporary accommodations while we search for a house, and school tuition for our daughter. They even offered an expensive car and a relocation allowance for me. That could have been what did it. At some point during the negotiations, he felt that he was being bought. The way they kept throwing more money into the offer made him upset. He wasn't for sale. He liked his job where he was, his colleagues, his laboratory, the classes he taught. He refused their offer." So what in, say, New York would have added to the job's attractiveness, in Bangkok was perceived as being an insult—illustrating how widely the value of a supposed reward can vary depending on a person's cultural assumptions.

come from an external source, and they are given by someone or the company in exchange for attaining a prespecified level of productivity or achievement. They are known as fringe benefits, perquisites, or perks, and they are aimed at increasing loyalty, energy, and enthusiasm. Common perks in the United States include take-home vehicles, hotel stays, free refreshments, leisure activities during work time (massages, golf, and so on), stationery, allowances for lunch, and the first choice for such things as job assignments and vacation scheduling. Employees may also be given the first chance at job promotions when vacancies exist.

Outside the United States, many of these so-called perks are sponsored by the government or mandatory in local labor laws. In this case, the perk becomes a prerequisite or an acquired right for performing a task or job. In countries where they are not part of the job description, the receiver may be subject to high personal taxes. These extrinsic motivators—whether they are subsidized by the government or organized by the company—are short-term energizers that lose their impact once they become measurable, repeatable, and reliable. The best extrinsic motivators are those that are the least expected.

Intrinsic rewards include the personal satisfaction of performing the task or job, the variety and autonomy in how the job is performed, and the internal sense of achievement the performer perceives in accomplishing the task. A positive social climate—giving the impression of being at a good place to work—is an intrinsic reward. These kinds of rewards are, as the saying goes, their own reward, because the person performing the job is the one determining the value of the reward. They are both the giver and receiver, the one who measures and perceives the worthiness of the reward. These kinds of rewards include taking on new challenges that when achieved give a person a sense of exceeding his or her capacity, or contributing to a charity that gives a sense of a personal accomplishment of giving back to society, which in turn brings pride to oneself, the team, and/or the company. People are more motivated by acts of altruism, social responsibility, and visions that lead them beyond their own individual needs and concerns. Finding ways to reward others gives us a richer and deeper sense of purpose.

Considerations for Offering Rewards

A fine line separates who we are—including our values, beliefs, and assumptions—and what we want, success and happiness. In the sidebar above, the global executive invested her passion and energy in her stressful and demanding job, and her expected reward, success, was the promotion—though she did not get it. In the sidebar about the professor above, the meaning wanted in return—happiness, as the by-product of his research, writing, publishing, and his relationships with colleagues and students—did not translate into a monetary transaction. So, if rewarding others is not simply just offering that cut-and-paste perk from the human resources manual, where are we headed in a flat, overpopulated, and imperfect globalized world?

We all look to achieve status in one form or another. Though modesty is valued in some cultures and self-promotion is valued in others, knowing when to recognize and how to reward others for their contributions is essential. Even in cultures where modesty is valued—as in many countries outside the United States—the need to be appreciated is human. One particularly apt example is Australia, where the "tall poppy" syndrome teaches people not to stick out above the rest, to cultivate an egalitarian attitude, and to avoid anything that could resemble bragging or self-promotion. Yet studies show that being recognized through positive feedback, being liked, having strong relationships, and achieving challenging goals—especially when they are noticed by the boss in public—overrides the personal desire to keep one's head down. This is when recognition becomes a reward.

The recent global recession, global outsourcing, and the global marketplace for talent have jeopardized the options of upward mobility and ever-increasing bonuses. Today, global organizations are facing the challenge of trying to keep levels of engagement high while balancing financial and nonfinancial rewards—the extrinsic and intrinsic rewards that are essential to keeping talented people on board.

People want to know how they are doing, so mastering the art of feedback is key to encouraging intrinsic rewards. Unexpected, symbolic extrinsic rewards in public settings, which include both the individual contributors and the entire team, remain motivating. An overall, integrated approach to striking the balance between intrinsic and extrinsic reward systems can be found in the four-R formula.

Applying the Four Rs to Rewards

To encourage, energize, and engage global workforces, I suggest that a combination of the four Rs provides a significant solution. You have learned that random acts of kindness, developing an attitude of gratitude, doling out the right amount of praise and thank-yous, and increasing the ties to the organization with a sense of belonging are specific actions you can take to promote the delicate balance within reward systems. Integrating these actions into the four-R formula will reinforce a deeper sense of appreciation, belonging, pride, and personal contribution to the vision and purpose of the global organization. When *respect* is shown, people are more attentive to each other, *relationships* become stronger, *recognition* leads to loyalty, and *rewards* develop commitment and integrity due to clearly defined and consistent behaviors. Let's explore how this can be done in practice.

First, respect can lead to rewards, because listening gets a quicker buy-in. For example, by being attentive and attuned to others, you are aware of their wants and desires. You can then choose the words that influence those inner feelings that make people feel good about themselves and help them see their role in the successful outcome.

Second, as relationships become stronger, collaboration becomes an intrinsic driver because people are responsible toward each other, and there is a natural support system in place that makes them want to work together. For example, when you know that you can rely on team members and other people in the organization, information is openly shared, and you want to keep people in the loop and avoid misunderstandings that can harm relationships.

Third, when a person is recognized, it makes him or her feel good. They naturally become more engaged in how they perform. For example, a simple gesture of appreciation makes you want to go the extra mile and give an extra ounce of energy, because, after all, we all like to be liked.

Fourth, when a reward is offered, what really matters is not necessarily what is offered but how and why. For example, leaving an expected bonus check at someone's disposal without a kind word of recognition, handshake, or sign of gratitude devalues the hard work and effort put into accomplishing the task. Compensation is meant as a source of short-term motivation; but inspiration is the long-lasting, meaningful, purpose-driven reason why we do what we do, for ourselves, for others, and for the organization.

This virtuous circle reinforces the reality of each of the four Rs, and thus increases the value of being listened to, the sense of belonging, and the rewarding contribution when we feel recognized for who we are, not only what we bring to the organization.

Rewards Across Cultures

People want to be rewarded tomorrow for what they contribute today. Even in countries whose political systems frown upon individualism and prevent achievement orientation, meritocracy is on the rise. To meet the challenges and opportunities that globalization is bringing to our door-step, high-performance organizations identify the need to adapt their culture to one that is results oriented, customer focused, and collaborative. Effective performance management systems can drive these strategic changes, yet they appear to be highly influenced by American value orientations (Chiang and Birtch 2006).

Despite the view that these values appear to be driven by U.S. cultural hegemony, the days when organizations could be run subjectively and ambiguously are over. Team members or leaders who rely on local and culture-specific status symbols or pass the buck one level up or down rigid hierarchal structures are becoming organizational dinosaurs. Cultural dimensions that refer to ascribed status-versus-achievement orientations are being left behind as meritocracy invades our daily personal and professional lives. This is reality in the global workforce.

In general, an effective performance management system is based on clear guidelines of competencies, values, and behaviors that demonstrate the vision and mission of the global organization. Employees need to know what is expected of them and how can they succeed in the organization. Knowing what is measured, how, when, on what conditions, and for what reasons lays the foundation for employee motivation and leads to engagement.

Being results oriented and customer focused is often considered an American value orientation. This orientation has been found to be dominant in global organizations because stockholders are no longer local, but it can also be problematic because stakeholders are most often not accustomed to management by objectives. Just as in the example of Emmanuel's story recounted in chapter 1, mistrust and misunderstandings need to be eliminated and not underestimated. Collaboration is a value that finds its origins in more relationship-oriented, in-group, and interdependent cultures. This shows that cross-fertilization is taking place in truly global organizations. Thus, we are witnessing the evolution of international organizations from those that run their operations from a centralized, national, monoculture headquarters to those that are globalized and network-centric. They need to follow procedures and policies that have standard frameworks but are locally customized, that welcome input from subsidiaries, and that encourage culturally diverse talent management and product innovation, which feed into and spur the organization's globally competitive edge.

Overall, then, those involved in devising rewards systems need to listen attentively to how policies and procedures are done both at home and abroad—what worked, what didn't, and what can willingly be done differently.

When recruiting in the global marketplace, understanding the values that are demonstrated by behaviors is essential so as not to make the mistake of hiring those who resemble us. Remember that if there are those who learn early on that self-promotion is a valued behavior, they will make the effort to be seen, heard, and accounted for. In corporate cultures where that is admired and expected, promotions and rewards may go to the exuberant overachiever. In corporate cultures where modesty and group harmony are valued behaviors, the more consensus-oriented listener is the one who is looked to and admired. When the more outspoken, competitive-spirited person is transferred overseas and finds that the local culture values the quiet-spoken, consensus attributes, he or she is shocked. The quest for the reward becomes ambiguous.

Taking initiative becomes a complicated cultural facet when being number one is not the name of the game. Thus, here are keys to establishing a corporate culture that identifies with the added value of diversity and the opportunities that globalization can bring to twenty-first-century organizations:

- understanding that cultural subtleties exist around the globe
- making sure that the corporate culture clearly identifies what is considered valued behaviors and nonnegotiable ones
- providing training and coaching for employees unaccustomed to or unaware of how these behaviors are portrayed.

No matter what the local cultural norm may be, all employees seek rewards that are most often found in the simple expression of appreciation, especially when it comes from the boss. Likewise, here are a few reward system reminders:

- Today, *not* to have a solid performance management system in place is scandalous—not only for the organization, whether it's public or private, but even more so out of respect for the employees—the stakeholders, not the stockholders—who value equality and fairness. Their expectations are intimately linked to the principles of reward and recognition.
- Understand that establishing standardized policies and procedures should be considered a framework, not a cut-and-paste application that can simply be imposed around the globe.
- Trust that employees do want to succeed and be rewarded. Investing in them as they learn to discover their strengths and adapt to the transitions and transformations that globalization requires of them as well as of the organization will not only add a measurable return-on-investment to the bottom line but an even bigger return on *expectations* as employee engagement increases.

Toward More Effective Multicultural Rewards Systems

With the recent global economic upheaval, the world has witnessed that American companies promoting reward systems designed to nurture excellence based on value orientations of unharnessed competition and purely self-directed individualism have actually fostered corruption and bad performance. Therefore, today's business world needs to shed former best practices and rethink compensation and performance-linked incentives in hopes of developing sustainable "next practices"—an amalgamation of the old and new, the East and West (Hampden-Turner and Trompenaars 2004), along with the integration of the four Rs—respect, relationships, recognition, and rewards.

The implications of this seismic shift in the globalized corporate environment vary widely from organization to organization—but they are obvious. It is beyond the scope of this book to try to suggest how this change could affect your particular organization. But I'm sure you can think of plenty of examples.

A Brief Look at the Science Behind Rewards

Before we move on, it's useful to take a brief look at the science behind rewards. Neuroscience researchers are studying the effects of reward responses, engagement, and mindfulness. People experience deep engagement when they experience a strong reward state. To understand reward responses, we need to understand the importance of dopamine, a powerful chemical neurotransmitter behind pleasure seeking. As explained in chapter 3, when you receive a reward, your brain is flooded with this feel-good neurotransmitter. If the rewards become commonplace, however, the level of dopamine released decreases. Pretty soon, there is no "high" associated with receiving the reward.

To understand how the brain reacts to rewards, we need to understand this dopamine rush, then distinguish the loss aversion rush (total letdown from not receiving reward) compared with the status quo bias, which is the routine of receiving a consistent, minimum reward (an example would be annual salary-based bonuses instead of variable stock options). Loss aversion is very strong—we don't like to lose, and that's why we hold on to stocks even if prices are falling (Lehrer 2009). The intensity of delayed gratification is tied to how much we lust after a reward and how well we can implement metacognition distracting techniques to avoid thinking about the reward. This was first noted in the 1970s, when studies done by Walter Mischel, a professor of psychology at Stanford University, recorded how four-year-old children delayed gratification of eating tempting candy and, years later, how these behaviors influenced their academic and professional success. The studies are continuing with the same participants who are now in their 40s. Results from brain scans are starting to show how neural circuitry influences our urges and our ability to control how we manage situations and think about rewards. It's no longer about pure intelligence or willpower but more about redirecting our initial desires and reactions to "won't power."

When evaluating levels of engagement, David Rock and Yiyuan Tang referred to a theory by the neuroscientist Evian Gordon whereby the brain organizes itself in such a way as to minimize danger and maximize reward as described in chapter 4. Using the SCARF model—status, certainty, autonomy, relatedness, and fairness (Rock 2008)—we learn that the levels of status, certainty, autonomy, relatedness, and fairness affect engagement. High levels of positive rewards in these domains will produce high levels of engagement.

The SCARF model can be further applied to the four Rs. As discussed in chapter 3 for the example of Maria in the Italian fashion industry, *authentic adaptation* means attentively listening to others and adapting our behaviors as a sign of respect, which promotes other people's *status*; clarity in communication reduces ambiguity, thus increasing *certainty*; *collaborative initiative* builds trust, as we can rely on others' collaborative spirit while maintaining a healthy level of self-initiative, thus giving us a sense of *autonomy* and *relatedness*; and finally *energetic empathy*—where we see and perceive worldviews through the eyes of others, acknowledge their perspectives, and understand how they feel without being drawn into their internal emotional conflicts—signals the emotion so dear to all of us: a feeling of *fairness*.

An even richer reward today is high performance in successful, multicultural teams working and collaborating around the globe. Regardless

of the acronym used, the four Rs—when integrated and applied authentically—are professionally beneficial across cultures and around the globe.

R R / R R Questions for Reflection and What's Next

This chapter's key points include how performance systems increase
engagement and bring clarity and transparency to global organizations.
Rewards are the expected result from successful outcomes. Everyone,
everywhere around the globe wants to be appreciated. Understanding the
subtle cultural norms that define the valued behaviors of reward systems
will increase understanding as employees recalibrate their cultural expectations while working and collaborating around the globe. The long-term
solution to employee engagement is to find the balance between those
extrinsic rewards given to us by others and those intrinsically rewarding
feelings that surge within us. If you think of well-being as an intrinsic
reward, I'd like to suggest that "well-doing" is an extrinsic reward.

Now consider these questions as "next practices," and find answers
that you can apply in the global workplace within your organization,
keeping in mind that much of the workforce is geographically dispersed
and virtually connected:

1. What rewards can be given in your organization to employees who
   practice *well-being?* These lead to healthy environments, less absenteeism, and positive emotions.
2. Beyond monetary compensation, what rewards can be given in
   your organization for employees who practice *well-doing?* Balancing
   efficiency and effectiveness is the characteristic of work well done.

Chapter 6 distills the various insights and techniques described
throughout the book to offer you a tool kit for collaborating across
cultures.

Skills for Collaborating Across Cultures

Hope has never trickled down. It has always sprung up.

—Studs Terkel

The quotation above reveals what is happening in today's glob-ally interconnected and interdependent world. In the spirit of the groundswell trend, we see people sharing in ways they've never done before. The global economy, with its financial crashes, and the global workplace, with its culture clashes, have increased the trend of people connecting with and depending on each other in efforts to go beyond the barriers humankind has built.

From news websites like www.digg.com to web tools like del.icio.us, from social networking sites like Twitter and Facebook to user-generated sites like YouTube and Wikipedia, we see interconnectivity abounding all around the globe. Even in China, where the government has blocked Facebook, you can still connect via a site called Kaixin (meaning "fun"), which is quite popular with working people, and there are also other similar sites, such as Chinaren (for schoolmates) and RenRen (for social networks) (these examples are offered thanks to my colleague in China, Alex Ma).

The desire to break down, break through, and break the mold will be the source of success for tomorrow. This can only happen if your connections include collaboration as a key ingredient. So once again, the four Rs come into play—respect, relationships, recognition, and rewards. To collaborate, you need to listen—the basic element of respect. You also need others—without which there are no relationships. Collaboration is about sharing, and you can only do so when it is appreciated—recognized. The reward comes for bringing together the knowledge, experience, and skills that each and every one of us has within.

In the next and final chapter, we'll look at the big picture of how to work effectively in the globalized workplace from the perspective of the four Rs. This chapter offers a short, practical supplement and tool kit—a handy summing up of the various insights and techniques described throughout the book for collaborating effectively across cultures. I've also added a few more pointers on how to engage employees effectively to pursue true cross-cultural collaboration.

Skills Related to Respect

Three types of skills are related to respect: those involving awareness, those involving attentiveness, and those that involve being adaptive. Let's briefly consider each.

Becoming More Aware

Two types of skills involve becoming more aware:

- Self-awareness: Reflect on how your actions and reactions influence verbal and nonverbal communication. You can no longer say "that's just the way I am." Self-awareness leads to self-development.

- Awareness of others: Ask yourself what is required in this context? With whom, and how?

Becoming More Attentive

Two types of skills involve becoming more attentive:

- Be attentive to yourself: Knowing what drives you (your values), what stories you tell yourself (your beliefs and assumptions), and how you project and what you expect are all part of how you are perceived.

- Be attentive to others: No matter how you want to be seen, the observer's perception of who he or she sees is accurate for that person. Getting the conversation going means being attentive to be more authentic. This is the first step in the process of authentic adaptation—finding comfort while continuously adapting to unfamiliar or foreign situations.

Becoming More Adaptive

Two types of skills involve becoming more adaptive:

- Learn to learn. In the words of Alvin Toffler (1970), "the illiterate of the 21st century will not be those who cannot read and write, but those who cannot learn, unlearn and relearn."

- Share lessons learned. Whenever we learn anything new, our primary reaction is that of discomfort. Avoid the blame game and accept that the discomfort is part of the learning curve. To be skillful in today's world, you need to go beyond living in the past, removing the historical handcuffs that prevent us from embracing change. Leave behind your former habit-driven, accepted ways of being tied to "this is just how we do things around here," and aim to find comfort in a constant state of transition and transformation.

Skills Related to Relationships

Three types of skills are related to relationships: those involving collaboration, those involving initiative, and those focusing on people. Let's briefly consider each.

Becoming More Collaborative

Two types of skills involve becoming more collaborative:

- Develop a collaborative spirit, where contributing early and often are key ingredients.
- Openly contribute toward a better outcome.

Taking More Initiative

Two key skills are related to taking more initiative:

- Encourage others to share knowledge and skills. If you take the lead, others will follow.
- Eliminate the fear-of-failure factor. Change and innovation can only occur if you challenge what you have always accepted as the only way or the right way of doing something.

Developing People Skills

Four types of skills involve focusing more on people:

- Trust more openly—remind yourself that without relationships, there is no collaboration.
- Count on people spontaneously. This is how we energize ourselves and others.
- Encourage autonomy—this is how we empower others and motivate in the short term.
- Be decisive—make those difficult decisions when it comes to accountability. This is how we engage others and inspire for the long term.

Skills Related to Recognition

Three types of skills are related to recognition: those involving energy, those involving empathy, and those involving emotions. Let's briefly look at each one.

Becoming More Energized

Three types of skills involve becoming more energized:

- Be positive—emotions are contagious.

- Be predictable—walk the talk.

- Make sure to practice the two skills above in tandem—recognition comes with the combination of predictability and trustworthiness.

Becoming More Empathetic

Two types of skills involve becoming more empathetic:

- Be attuned to the context in which you find yourself. Do not just look; observe. Do not just hear; listen. Do not just think; feel.

- Shift your perspective from selfish wants and desires to the selfless needs of others.

Acknowledging Emotions

Two types of skills involve acknowledging emotions:

- Recognize what triggers your emotions. Learn to speak about your emotions, and appreciate them. Controlling them will come naturally if they are allowed to exist. Suppressing them is not only unhealthy but also ineffective. Repressed emotions always have a way of reappearing when we least expect or want them.

- Acknowledge the emotions of others. To turn off the emotional hijacking caused by physiological responses, you need to turn on the cognitive (thinking) process—open-ended questions starting with what, how, and when are the brakes to an emotional onslaught.

Skills Related to Rewards

Two types of skills are related to rewards, those involving well-being, and those involving well-doing. Here are a few pointers for each.

Focusing on Well-Being

Three types of skills involve well-being:

- Take care of yourself. Good health is the ultimate reward. It allows us not only to live longer and happier lives but also to be more productive and to more effectively interact with the world around us.

- Take care of those you love. Be mindful of others.

- You can only make others happy if you are happy. Practice secular mindfulness. Mindfulness, the opposite of being mindless, leads to enhanced well-being. By concentrating on the present and focusing on the moment at hand, you can learn to deal with the past and prepare for the future—and, as a by-product rather than something consciously sought, receive a gift: a sense of happiness.

Focusing on Well-Doing

Two types of skills involve well-doing:

- Take your job seriously, not yourself.

- Learn to recognize potential in yourself and in others, and then expect the best to emerge.

Miscellaneous Skills

A few more skills and tools cut across the four Rs—those related to communicating around the globe, to collaborating in the global workplace, and to celebrating for virtual and geodispersed teams. Let's consider each one.

Communicating Around the Globe

Diversity Icebreaker (DI), an assessment tool from the Oslo-based firm Human Factors AS, uses a seminar process to help people become more aware of the effect of categorization on perception, interaction, and group dynamics. In diversity management, DI is used to create shared mental models of what is needed to make diversity add value. Within

DI's strong emotional and humor-oriented experiential learning process, it is much easier to find the openness needed to be able to dive into more tricky areas of diversity, like cultural/disciplinary/gender issues.

DI includes a two-page self-report questionnaire (available in 19 languages), personal workbooks, a manual, a DVD, and an academic/practitioner book (Ekelund and Langvik 2008). These materials can all be purchased from Human Factors AS (www.human-factors.no).

Collaborating in the Global Workplace

Collaborative Teamwork is a tool developed by Kenneth A. Crow, the president of DRM Associates, a management consulting and education firm based in Palos Verdes, just south of Los Angeles, that specializes in new product development (www.npd-solutions.com). In its extensive experience with many kinds of firms, DRM has found ways to encourage collaboration, which requires effective teamwork. Team members must trust and respect one another. There must be open communication and a willingness to accept input from others. Teamwork often encounters conflicting goals; therefore, decision making must be based on a collaborative approach. This process is shown in figure 6-1.

DRM has found that many people believe that the ideal workplace strategy is compromise—which represents a moderate degree of both assertiveness and cooperativeness, the approach of "sometimes I win, and sometimes I lose." But compromise is not the ideal. A good team includes people who have strong beliefs and are professionally committed to the team's members. They also want a high degree of cooperation. This provides the basis for a collaborative approach—which means aiming for a "win–win" outcome. And as figure 6-1 illustrates, the key to reaching this outcome is to creatively search for solutions that can mutually satisfy the needs of all the team's members rather than focusing on just two competing solutions that involve trade-offs or are mutually exclusive.

Celebrating for Virtual and Geodispersed Teams

With geographically dispersed global teams, face-to-face celebrations are not often possible. Yet celebrating small wins, majors gains, and milestones strengthens the team's spirit. Some possibilities for doing so in spite

Figure 6-1. A Model of How Collaboration Works in the Global Workplace

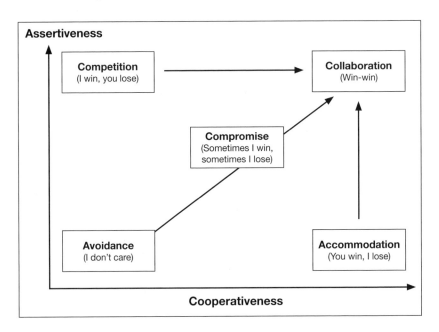

Note: This model represents two axes: cooperativeness and assertiveness. Different approaches to dealing with an issue are mapped against these two axes. A low degree of assertiveness and cooperativeness represents avoidance of an issue, or the approach of "I don't care." A high degree of cooperativeness and a low degree of assertion represent accommodation, or the approach of "You win, I lose." A high degree of assertiveness and a low degree of cooperativeness represent competition, or the approach of "I win, you lose."

of dispersion include the following (these ideas are from LinkedIn's Q&A section, www.linkedin.com—thanks to all the people around the globe):

- Set aside a day for the team to work on something of its choice. Make it creative and innovative—something that appeals to the team's strengths (artistic for design teams, inventive for engineering teams, and the like).

- Let the team members choose and participate in a project for a global charity.

- Have a virtual team gaming day with everyone's favorite video games.

- Send worldwide recognition emails across the company, and give token memorabilia (T-shirt, key ring) and $50 to each team member. Then they can choose locally how they prefer to spend the money—dinner out together or privately with family.

- Upload pictures and videos—using an Internet tool like Yammer or iChat or an intranet team space.

- Write a collective poem or short story with the highs and the lows of the team's time together.

- Record a song—silly or serious, but everyone sings a few words; and if everyone agrees, put it on YouTube.

- What *not* to do: Nothing.

- What you *should* do: Ask all the team's members how they want to celebrate.

What's Next

In chapter 7, we'll look at the four-R action plan for working effectively around the globe.

The Four-R Action Plan for Working Effectively Around the Globe

What if the next best thing to building a better world was simply creating a better workplace—an interconnected, globally dispersed environment where people come together via traditional and not-so-traditional means, where respect builds relationships, and where random acts of recognition lead to mutually rewarding interactions?

—Christopher, an engineer in a global organization

Think of a time of significant challenge or transition in your life. More than likely, your friends and family helped you through it. That's universal—as we encounter transitions and challenges in our lives, we need the support of a variety of people. People who respect us and people whom we respect.

As our world continues to shrink, moreover, our interdependence becomes increasingly more important and more enriching. Finding this place where the richness of each of our experiences, thoughts, creativity, new solutions to problems, breakthrough ideas, and other great opportunities combine—this is the future. It is the attainment of being culture savvy. Life is an exciting journey—no one said it is an easy one.

Therefore, in this chapter we consider the four-R action plan for how people from various cultures can learn to work together effectively. Living in a world where people from all cultures interact with and react comfortably to each other, we must develop more meaningful relationships and a worthwhile action plan. Things are changing, and for the better. In today's new leaders, we are witnessing people who balance various styles and adapt to behaviors without needing to adopt foreign behaviors.

This reality of this new leadership is illustrated by a recent article in the *New York Times* by Anand Giridharadas (2010). The author gives the examples of Indra Nooyi, an American citizen born in India who is the chairwoman of PepsiCo; U.S. president Barack Hussein Obama; Carlos Ghosn, the French-Lebanese-Brazilian executive who runs both a French automaker (Renault) and a Japanese one (Nissan); and Mohammed ElBaradei, the Egyptian international civil servant and Nobel laureate; as well as others beyond the spotlight—in firms, civic groups, and governments. As the author notes, "These cultural hybrids tend to avoid the traditional leader's need to declaim and set the agenda. They listen zealously and lead by empathy. They allow others to feel heard. Their eyes can dwell on the least included person in the room, perhaps because they, too, have known exclusion."

The four-R universal principles—respect, relationships, recognition, and rewards—are connected; you can't give, receive, or maintain one without integrating all four. The gift of respect—an act of esteem—is rewarding. Relationships cannot be formed without respect, and, in and of themselves, are rewards for being open and communicative. Recognition cannot occur without respect and relationships. In addition, being recognized is rewarding, because it reinforces the fact that others acknowledge us as humans and our contributions as valuable. Thus, the integration of these four universal principles makes it easier to cross cultural and linguistic barriers. Although cultures differ in how they show respect, form relationships, and recognize and reward people, in every culture these principles are the driving force behind working and collaborating more effectively around the globe.

From Barriers to Bridges

So what steps can you take to bring down the barriers to crossing cultural and linguistic divides? First, you need to stop referring to them as barriers—instead, reframe these challenges as resistance that you've built in your head. Then, you can begin to break down this resistance by changing the thoughts that come to mind when you first encounter what is different, foreign, or unfamiliar. Once you can savor the exotic and unexpected experiences that come your way, your facade melts and your heart opens.

Today, we all work with others from different cultures. Transnational interactions are here to stay. Multicultural neighborhoods, teams, and companies are commonplace. Some of us will have the opportunity to pursue an international assignment in a foreign country; many of us, without ever leaving home, will meet and work with people from different cultures in our neighborhoods, through customer service call centers, and local workplaces. It's surprising that even with this knowledge, companies in 2010 are still creating diversity departments in hopes of including those who are "different."

It's time to get in touch with reality. Take a few minutes to view a video on YouTube about how things are changing so fast in this digital age (www.youtube.com/watch?v=emx92kBKads). This may very well be the wake-up call to comprehend just how much the world is changing. We are living in times of exponential change. This is not to arouse fear but, instead, to bring into perspective this amazing reality. Are we ready to change with the world?

A quotation from the Dalai Lama sums it up nicely: "Under the bright sun, many of us are gathered together with different languages, different styles of dress, even different faiths. However, all of us are the same in being humans, and we all uniquely have the thought of 'I,' and we're all the same in wanting happiness and in wanting to avoid suffering."

A Personal Action Plan

Consider this: Along the United States–Mexico border, core border cultures, or *fronterizos* (borderlanders), are now transforming the landscape.

While both nation-states continue to exist with all their disparate political, economical, social, and cultural identities, the people known as border-landers have learned to blend the structures, institutions, and life expres-sions of the two societies to create something novel and entirely theirs: the *ambiente fronterizo*, or borderlands milieu.

Elsewhere, in northeastern Poland near the Lithuanian border, a small town named Sejny launched the Borderland Foundation in 1991. The foundation's main objective is to develop everyday practices that create open communities in areas where different national, ethnic, reli-gious, and cultural minorities coexist, and to find and develop means to preserve traditional cultures, and sometimes also minority cultures. The main street, with its White Synagogue, recalls the town's Jewish presence; the little evangelical church reminds us of the town's Protestants. The Polish and Lithuanian presence is a reality in today's Sejny. In the vicinity of the town, one can also find many traces of Russian "Old Believers," and if you move further to the south and to the east, you find more vast territories of cultural interpretation—Tartar, Karaite, and Armenian districts, all with residents from Belarus and Ukraine. Here, as in many towns and cities around the globe, people are trying to gather the wisdom and richness of borderlands—a wealth that results from the coexistence of different traditions and beliefs. We can do likewise as we work and col-laborate around the globe (Borderland Foundation 2010).

Only by going beyond the surface differences, and digging down to find the qualities that bring us together as humans, can we break down barriers and build the bonds so essential in today's world. Let's learn from others—like the borderlanders—about how they have successfully crossed the divides, built those bridges, and now have an enriched life and a deeper meaning of what it is to be human. Here's how to start—a four-step process to achieve success in a changing world:

- First, *acknowledge* that there will be challenges. Write them down on Post-its or index cards as you experience them. Look at your answers to worksheet 1-1, the Cultural Framework Survey, in chapter 1. Identify the different choices you and others have made. This should assist you in proactively addressing chal-lenges before they become sources of resistance.

- Second, *evaluate* your expectations to refocus your perspectives. Refer back to worksheet 2-1, the Cultural Values List Exercise, in chapter 2. Remind yourself that values are your foundation—your guides as you go forward—giving you direction, not moral definition. Know how you live your values—the behaviors that define them.

- Third, *celebrate* the large and small wins, and dispose of the Post-it notes and index cards on which you listed the challenges you were experiencing. Shift your perspective, change your worldview, and focus on cultivating an attitude of gratitude—it will physiologically change your brain.

- And fourth, *remain* open to what is new. Put yourself in situations that expand, not just stretch, your comfort zone. This will likely result in new challenges—and then you can begin the process again.

A Professional Action Plan

Likewise, your professional action plan includes the elements of reviewing, regulating, and evaluating. You will first need to think back on your career. Ask yourself: Where am I today? Where do I want to be tomorrow? And now take three steps.

First, *review* how your own culture influences who you are and how you do things—your behaviors. Culture is deep within us and difficult to define. One of the best ways is by trying to examine cultural artifacts in your environment, your organization, and your team. By being attentive to other people and their behaviors, you will bring life to your own values, attitudes, and assumptions. Ask yourself: What triggers the feelings of right and wrong? Then remind yourself that cultures are not right or wrong, only made up of learned and ingrained behaviors (how you do things) and logic (how you think about things) within an environment.

Then take the initiative to bring people together and have a high-quality conversation about *the* core value that we all have within us: the need to feel valued. Opening up and listening to another person's feelings is a sign of respect. This is the first step to enabling ourselves and others to move toward collaborating more effectively together. This is how we learn to understand how people feel and how they perceive their world. Empathy is all about sharing and acknowledging other people's perspectives. This leads to well-being, which in turn develops well-doing.

Second, *regulate*—learn to adapt but still remain authentic, and thus build trust and credibility. By listening to others with your heart, and acknowledging their rightful emotions, you start to think about what you are feeling. You encourage others to share their feelings. Self-reflection calms down the emotional hijacking, especially in times of a crisis or increased stress. Empathy translates into energy, empowerment, and engagement. Through the practice of mindfulness—the ability to be attuned to your environment, being aware of how you fit in and how you influence others through your verbal and nonverbal behaviors by simply being in the present—you will find the balance between being focused and being involved. Being supportive of others and attentive to your own well-being makes people feel valued, and this in turn drives performance, the very essence of well-doing.

Third, *recalibrate*—take steps to increase your self-awareness by identifying cultural influences, starting with a country-specific profile. Do a profile of the country from which you hold your passport. This will give you a snapshot of how you compare with what are considered your country's specific cultural dimensions. This helps bring self-awareness to your consciousness—it helps inform you of how you may or may not be aligned with the research and country-specific profiles that denote your national culture of origin. Developing self-awareness leads to self-development. You will be able to question the data about the country with which you most identify, and get a deeper understanding of your own core beliefs and behaviors—where you are aligned, and where you are not.

In this respect, there are many tools on the market, but one that is particularly well adapted to the business context is ArgonautOnline (www.argonautonline.com), an Internet-based cultural work-style assessment and resource library of more than 65 cultures that ties theory to practice and is based on research about real workplace challenges. When a user has completed its cultural assessment, Argonaut produces an easy-to-understand graphical map of that person's profile, which can be compared with any of the cultures in its database. The learner can immediately identify the areas for greatest attention (for an example, see figure 7-1).

Argonaut offers strategies for adapting to another culture as well as interactive exercises, quizzes, and tutorials. The tool also generates team profiles and suggests strategies for building trust and performance within diverse teams. If you would like to try Argonaut, simply send an email to service@argonautonline.com, and an Argonaut team member will reply with instructions. ASTD Press and I have arranged with Argonaut to offer free limited access to the readers of this book.

Figure 7-1. A Screenshot of an Argonaut Map of a Person's Cultural Profile

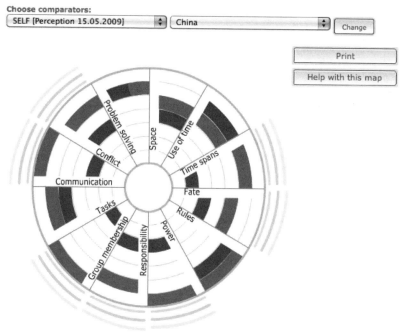

Note: See the text for an explanation of this map.

Source: Used by permission of ArgonautOnline (www.argonautonline.com).

Tools for Setting Thoughts in Motion

Think back on your career. Write down three to five developmental events or experiences, on or off the job, where you spontaneously learned competencies that you still use or a job you still do today. These opportunities for self-development have led you to expand your comfort zone, while using your innate talents.

Now identify those skills and competencies that you need to develop in today's global workplace. Which ones are best aligned with your inner talents? How can you and your colleagues acquire these competencies? Recent research has further verified the obvious reality that there are many factors to take into account when evaluating competencies for success in adapting to new and foreign environments—personality, gender, and experience variations are just a few examples. Role requirements for being effective internationally vary widely, and success may be determined on these factors as well.

With these criteria in mind, WorldWork Ltd. (www.worldwork.biz) specializes in the creation of tools to support managers involved in international transitions, namely, the transfer of professional skills into less-familiar cultural contexts. One of these tools, the International Profiler, a web-based psychometric questionnaire and personal feedback process, reveals the relative emphasis, attention, and energy individuals bring to a set of 10 international competencies with 22 dimensions representing associated skills, attitudes, and areas of knowledge; these have been adapted in worksheet 7-1. This worksheet enables you to do an exercise that can help you reflect on how global your mindset is. It gives you the opportunity to evaluate some of the competencies included in the International Profiler. This questionnaire is based on a five-rater Likert scale (a common psychometric scale in questionnaires) containing an overview of certain competencies found in the International Profiler. The full World-Work tool is far more complete and complex. (For further information on how to use this tool, contact www.worldwork.biz.)

Worksheet 7-1. Thinking Globally: Interpersonal Skills in an Intercultural World

Self-Evaluation: How Global Is Your Mindset?

Choosing 1 shows you do not agree at all. By choosing 6, you agree entirely with the statement; 0 is no opinion or not applicable.

Skill	0	1	2	3	4	5	6
I am open to new ideas, new ways of doing things. I easily build relationships with people who have attitudes and behaviors different from mine.							
I am interested in learning other languages, and understand the difficulty when others speak a language that is not native to them.							
I listen more than I talk, and I adapt my language accordingly and am attuned to other people's nonverbal communication styles.							
I am an attentive listener. When absorbing new information, I check it with what I already know, check my perception of what the other person is saying or not saying, and then, and only then, do I predict what will happen next.							
I am flexible in that I reflect on situations, reframe them in their situational context, and am able to adapt my behaviors, question my assumptions, and modify any preconceived ideas I may have about certain people.							

The higher the score, the more adaptable you will be when working and living in today's global environments.

Worksheet 7-1 (*continued*)

Self-Evaluation: How Globally Minded Am I?

Choosing 1 shows you do not agree at all. By choosing 6, you agree entirely with the statement; 0 is no opinion or not applicable.

Skill	0	1	2	3	4	5	6
I am aware of the values that drive and motivate me. My values are defined by my behaviors. With these as my guide, I cope with external forces that could prevent me from reaching my goals when situations can be stressful.							
I take initiatives yet accept that interdependence and shared responsibility go with accountability.							
I believe the key to trust across cultures is accomplished through respect and relationships. Building this takes time, sensitivity to context, and a range of styles to adapt to various environments (formal/informal, hierarchal/flat matrix, and the like).							
With the intent of creating innovative alternative solutions, I strive for synergy in decision making, as well as in complex and creative problem solving.							
When it comes to recognizing and rewarding myself and others, I know that purely monetary acknowledgment is short term. To inspire, we need to be more collaborative in both our personal and professional lives.							

The higher the score, the more adaptable you will be when working and living in today's global environments.

Source: Inspired by the International Profiler by WorldWork (www.worldwork.biz). Used by permission.

The International Profiler is a psychometric developmental tool that combines employees' self-awareness and cultural competencies to create an organizational plan. The creators of this tool have asked:

- What makes an individual highly effective in transferring individual skills to an unfamiliar, cross-cultural context?
- How can we identify potential skill gaps for a target group of individuals?

Although each individual's profile is different and should reflect the specific role and/or contextual challenges that the person faces, the International Profiler database reveals primary success factors through the prioritization of competencies of international managers and professionals. Figure 7-2 shows the 22 skills, attitudes, and areas of knowledge grouped into 10 competencies and regrouped into subcategories. These competencies determine success in foreign or unfamiliar environments. The two primary sets are called push and pull competencies. "Push" competencies refer to a person's proclivity to push their ideas out in a clear, easily understood manner (an "inside/out" approach). "Pull" competencies, on the other hand, refer to an "outside/in" approach. These people tend to pull others' worlds and perspectives into their own before formulating and disseminating an idea. The results show that professionals who have lived abroad give significantly more emphasis to "pull' areas of competence; those who have never lived abroad give more emphasis to the "push" competencies. The other three sets of competencies are leading across cultures, communication, and cultural knowledge.

The International Profiler helps organizations and employees to assess where they focus their energy today, to compare this focus with those of other international professionals, and to track the changes over time as international experience increases. The results of the International Profiler also suggest that people with expatriate experience are more likely to have developed certain leadership skills, including the ability to draw on a range of styles when influencing others and the ability to solve problems creatively. With this tool, organizations can better identify where their employees' focus their energies and how they can more effectively assemble teams and assign projects.

Figure 7-2. The Range of Intercultural Competencies

PULL COMPETENCIES	PUSH COMPETENCIES	LEADING ACROSS CULTURES
1. Openness New thinking Welcoming strangers Acceptance *2. Flexibility* Flexible behavior Flexible judgment Learning languages	*3. Personal autonomy* Inner purpose Focus on goals *4. Emotional strength* Resilience Coping Spirit of adventure	*9. Influencing* Rapport Range of styles Sensitivity to context *10. Synergy* Creating new alternatives
COMMUNICATION *5. Perceptiveness* Attuned Reflected awareness *6. Listening orientation* Active listening *7. Transparency (push)* Clarity of communication Exposing intentions	**CULTURAL KNOWLEDGE** *8. Cultural knowledge* Information gathering Valuing differences	

Note: See the text for an explanation of this listing.

Source: Inspired by the International Profiler by WorldWork (www.worldwork.biz). Used by permission.

Summing Up

The journey on which we have embarked throughout this book—toward the unification of heart, head, and mind—is coming to an end here, but not elsewhere. We have looked at our new, interconnected, and globalized workplace, which has forced us to explore cultural values, personal perceptions, global perspectives, and corporate dilemmas. We have learned about the four Rs that unite us—our needs to feel respected, to build relationships, and to be recognized and rewarded. In the appendix that follows this last chapter, I share success stories from people around the globe who, when learning about the book, wanted to be part of the celebration. The general feeling is that the world is changing and will continue to do so at exponential rates. Quantum leaps will be sudden for those unprepared or unwilling to change. Preparing ourselves, and our organizations, will prevent a revolution and enable more peaceful evolution.

You are unique. I am unique. We each have something to offer the world. Like diamonds in the rough, treasure the different facets of each individual. You and I can make a difference in the world by no longer looking for differences in others. The change that is happening is with the meaningful purpose of bringing people together. Borderless countries, flattened hierarchies, and interconnected people are bringing down artificial walls and barriers built out of fear. Scratch the surface of the next person you meet; reach out and get to know him or her by listening with all your heart, head, and mind.

R R
R R Questions for Reflection

Consider these questions:

1. What will our world look like tomorrow, when we change our personal perspectives and professional priorities?
2. What can you do differently to influence the world for a better tomorrow? A video on YouTube of a 12-year-old who silenced the world for five minutes can lead to deeper reflection (www.youtube .com/watch?v=TQmz6Rbpnu0).

Appendix: Success Stories of People Working and Collaborating Around the Globe

These stories, as with the many short stories in this book, help us to identify the steps taken by others in their attempts to bridge cultural and linguistic divides. The first step to successfully integrating cultures in our everyday lives is assessing our values. When what we consider valuable in our life's journey becomes clear, we can more purposefully illustrate our values through behavior. If we can clearly define where we are headed and what we want in the bigger picture of life, we can build deeper relationships, based on trust and reliability. Self-awareness makes us more adaptive; when we know our strengths, we become better prepared for the ups and downs that life and relationships will bring, and, in turn, develop emotional intelligence.

As we go through life, each and every one of us wants to be recognized and rewarded. As in Warren and Fernando's story of a successful partnership, we see that acknowledging differences is rewarding each of us for being unique. Agreeing to disagree invites innovation and creation as we build new and multiple perspectives. We learn to solve problems better and proactively. It is no coincidence that SAS, the world's largest privately held software business, was voted the best company to work for, as reported by *Fortune* magazine in February 2010. Its CEO, Jim Goodnight, gets the fact that individuals are valuable—and should be recognized and rewarded. He is quoted as saying: "My chief assets drive out the gate every day. My job is to make sure they come back."

Let's look at some people's advice and experience on how they have been successful. Perhaps, we, too, can learn from them, share their emotions and become global citizens.

One caveat: These stories epitomize, in various ways, the four Rs—respect, relationships, recognition, and rewards. And the storyteller may even refer to a particular R. But because these stories recount the complexity of everyday life, in general, they cannot be easily categorized as pertaining to one R as distinct from another. So read and enjoy them, and apply their multifarious lessons.

My Culture, by Agnes Mura, CEO, Mura and Associates

My "culture" is that of a repeat immigrant. I escaped Communist Romania in my late teens, equipped with an excellent, values-based multilingual education and nothing else. I always defend the values of the countries or regions I know against the snap judgments of the place I find myself in. Having to culturally adjust to Western Europe and then to the U.S. southwest has been tremendously expansive. The extreme degree to which I still value [portable] education of the mind and heart has formed how I relate to, manage, and coach people.

A Story about the United States, by Glen Cooper

My culture, "American" culture, seems to me like a big tossed salad. Depending upon what kind of bite you take, the flavor and texture can be quite varied: sometimes bitter, sometimes sweet, and everything else in between! I love the America that we are still becoming—mixing every culture in a free and freewheeling complexity that never stops changing. Our founding fathers and mothers would be fascinated at what and who we are. As the world now gets to encounter us more closely with the direct contact we now all enjoy more and more, I actually think they will like us better and that we will like others better. I am very hopeful for the future. I believe we are finally coming together as a world village.

The Story of a Successful Partnership, by Fernando Espinosa, Senior Managing Partner, Qualifind, Inc., Professional and Executive Search

My partner, Warren Carter, at Qualifind Executive Search, is originally from a little town called Blackshear in Georgia (about three hours north of Jacksonville). I was born and raised in a suburb of Mexico City. We have completely different backgrounds and are quite opposite, yet we have been able to create a wonderful partnership. We never fight, we have complete trust in each other, and we care for one another like brothers.

How did all this begin? We used to be competitors in the executive search business in the United States–Mexico border region of Tijuana and San Diego. One day we had an opportunity to talk further and get to know each other better. We decided to join forces and become partners in December 1999. We have been together for 10 years and have survived several ups and downs in our industry. Warren is also a cancer survivor and is always ready to give his best as a professional and as a human being.

The main reason for our successful partnership is that we acknowledge our differences in personality, background, and culture. This acknowledgment makes us conscious of the fact that we need to look at things through our partner's eyes.

The second reason for our successful relationship is mutual understanding. We don't try to force things. We do our best in trying to understand why each one of us reacts the way we do and we don't judge each other.

The third aspect that supports the success of our partnership is our mutual respect. When things don't work out as we expect, or when we have a disagreement, before engaging ourselves in the typical finger-pointing routines, we focus as a team on finding the best potential solution to the problem. Once we achieve that, then we try to figure out what happened, how it happened, and how to avoid it from happening again.

And, last but not least, we try to adapt to one another. We know that there are hundreds of things that make us very different. In fact, we agree to disagree and, because of that, we are always trying to problem solve instead of persuade the other to see things our way. We use and enforce each other's strengths and supplement each other's weaknesses.

A Story by Vinay Kumar, Born in India and Living in the United States

In an Indian village, some villagers define success as having a certain amount of land and cows. In an American city, some define it as having a big home and fancy cars. To others, success is defined by education and degrees. Ultimately, after spending years trying to meet others' definitions of success, and being caught in a cycle of attainment and disappointment, I have come to realize that success has less to do with external achievement and more to do with an internal state of being. To me, the ultimate measure of success is if we are happy. If we're happy, then we're successful. If not, then no matter how much we have accumulated, in my eyes, we have failed. I have experienced and observed that all humans share common intrinsic motivators, regardless of our culture, origin, career choice, type of organization within which we work, our title, gender, socioeconomic class, and other surface differences. And when we express them, we feel energized and happy. I travel around the globe, have worked cross-culturally, and have family members from various places. I find that aside from the surface differences we're, in essence, all the same. When we communicate and interact from that deep authentic human place within us, we come to realize we're all one.

What keeps us from realizing that oneness and communicating authentically, however, is the stereotypical images we carry within. For example, all Indians are engineers and doctors, the British are stiff, the French are slackers, African Americans are great dancers, and all Americans are pushy. To be totally candid, I, too, used to have such preconceived images. I came to realize, however, that to put entire groups of people into such confining boxes was wrong. There are all kinds of people everywhere. Once I realized this, I began to look at each individual for who they are as a person and what makes them special.

A Story by Marie Brice, Born in New Zealand and Living in Texas; Owner of Zencompass

During my two years in Bombay as a Kiwi/Australian expat, I worked with an amazing group of 25 young people who had been selected from 300 hopefuls to become sponsored teaching fellows. These young people hailed from some of the poorest conditions in Bombay and they were all destined to go back to their communities and "be the change" in educating young children. Chronically monolingual, I struggled for the first few months as our shared language of "English" was surprisingly different.

However, a mutual respect for what we all held in common—our love of teaching and children—helped get us started. It was not long before I realized that the relationships we were developing wound deeper than the content we were sharing. This extended into a shared love of music—something not common in early childhood education in India. Recognizing this bond, this way that music connected our cultures and spirits was to turn into musical journey that now sees my Akanksha fellows sharing Maori, Australian, and English songs and music with children all over Bombay's poorest slums. I will never forget when one of my students had her class sing "Ke hite tuna" (a Maori children's song from New Zealand) for me at a school open day! My "kids" still write to me often and share their own successes, even though we now live far away in Texas. . . . And here? Well, I am singing in a classic rock band.

Success across Cultures, by Margarita Gokun Silver

My experience has been that when I listen to people—and I mean, really listen—I establish relationships, create connections, and move forward in a new culture in a much easier and more congruent way. By really listening, I mean listening between the lines, listening for what makes that person tick, listening for what moves them, listening for what's important to them—and listening to all that without any judgments and/or assumptions. Once I get the sense of who they are by using this kind of powerful listening, I move forward in my relationship with them by respecting their aspirations and goals and looking for ways for us to work together in such a way that they get to honor those aspirations and goals.

What's in a Name? A Story by Peter Hayward

We often cover our own embarrassment by laughing, brought on by the fact that we have made an error that opens us up to ridicule, so we deflect the ridicule on to the one who exposed us. Case in point: When among a homogeneous group, someone is introduced to the group who has a heavy accent or whose name is "unpronounceable," the outsider is made to bear the blunt of the ridicule.

"Suzie" was an Amer-Asian teenager from Vietnam who resettled in the United States. She quickly discovered to be accepted by her teenage peers she needed to fit in. After initially introducing herself as Minwit, she found herself dubbed "Nitwit," "dimwit," "witless" by others, teachers and teens who saw no harm in denigrating her name. Trying to fit in, she changed her name to Suzie, but remained shy and withdrawn. She even found herself alienated from her own family as she ignored her cultural background and tried to be more American.

One day, Debbie, an American native, who had lived and worked in Vietnam met Suzie. After discovering her real name and reason for her adopted name Debbie starting using the Suzie's birth name Minwit and began to show respect to Minwit's cultural background. Soon Minwit was acting more confident, outgoing—she showed pride in her cultural and family back ground. Her performance in school and work improved significantly and she found she had more friends than ever before.

To this day, I make it an important part of any team building that each team member learns to correctly pronounce each other's name and to learn about each other's cultural background. Out of mutual respect comes trust which leads to a work situation where team members feel comfortable advocating different perspectives. This creates a cohesive, supportive and productive team.

A Story by Helene Honeybone, Practical Advertising, Dallas–Fort Worth

As a native Swede, while working as a manager for a large corporation in Texas, I quickly had to learn to recognize intercultural differences both in myself and in others. While recognizing and respecting the differences in management styles for example, I had to be fast and straightforward in communications and structured and effective in decision-making situations, but I also felt a need to teach the group I worked with that the Swedish way of cooperating and problem solving as a team has its clear advantages.

I believe that my success was helped by the fact that I had previously lived and worked in cultures that were even more different than Texas, Singapore included. However, I also believe that I was able to be successful because of an open mind and no set expectations. I was aware that management styles in Texas can be different from Sweden, and I was prepared to mix in the new culture with my own in order to reach the common goal.

A Story by Theresa Ip Froehlich, Life Coach, Soar-by-Design Coaching

I was born and raised in Hong Kong by parents who spoke no English. Being married to a Caucasian American, I also work with bicultural issues in the home.

In building cross-cultural relationships, we must begin with checking our own attitudes. We can show respect for others only if we have that attitude of respect inside of us. In relating to people from other cultures, I show respect by initiating conversations and listening well, being willing to wait for them to speak their minds and their hearts even when they are struggling with their English. Respect expressed through humble listening then builds trust. In so many ways, the relationship and the trust are the rewards.

I think you hit the nail in the head with your third R—recognition. I have personally heard some immigrants in the United States complain that their contributions are not being recognized in the workplace or even churches where native white Americans are the majority. To recognize their ideas, contributions, and simply participation is to recognize their humanity as being equal to our humanity—to recognize that they are visible and real human beings! It is so basic.

A Story by Grace Doris

I think "self and other-awareness" is the breeding ground for building respect for those who are different to us and whose behavior is motivated by a different set of values and beliefs from ours. To start with, helping someone become aware that their beliefs and values are located on a continuum and not necessarily just "normal" helps them to then make the journey towards realizing that those who are different are not "wrong" but just different. And while we all have our preferences and that will not easily change, we can bring balance to our own point of view by adding the benefits of the opposite viewpoint.

At the moment, I am living this out in my current job, where my boss is a big-picture person, and her strengths lie in different areas to mine. However together, we make a strong team and cover all the areas of work that need to be done. I focus on the finance and the details and she looks after policy and planning. Initially, she and I found it difficult to like each other as we were so different, but eventually we both came to appreciate the other person's strengths and put aside our opinion that the other person was wrong just because they were different to us. I have also taken on board her attitude to take life a bit easy, and so have reduced my stress levels, and she has increased her attention to detail as she has come to see the value in doing that in her own work, too.

References

APS News (American Physical Society). 2003. This Month in Physics History: Circa January 1961—Lorenz and the Butterfly Effect. www.aps.org/publications/apsnews/200301/history.cfm.

Bingham, Tony, and Marcia Conner. 2010. *The New Social Learning: A Guide to Transforming Organizations Through Social Media.* Alexandria, VA, and San Francisco: ASTD Press and Berrett-Kohler.

Borderland Foundation. 2010. Borderland. http://pogranicze.sejny.pl/archiwum/english/found/found.htm.

Cacioppo, J.T., and B. Patrick. 2008. *Loneliness: Human Nature and the Need for Social Connection.* New York: W. W. Norton.

Carey, Benedict. 2007. Brain Injury Said to Affect Moral Choices. *New York Times*, March 22.

Carter, E.J., and K.A. Pelphrey. 2008. Friend or Foe? Brain Systems Involved in the Perception of Dynamic Signals of Menacing and Friendly Social Approaches. *Journal of Social Neuroscience* 3: 151–63.

Chiang, Flora F.T., and Thomas A. Birtch. 2006. An Empirical Examination of Reward Preferences within and across National Settings. *Management International Review*, November 1.

Copeland, Lennie, and Lewis Griggs. 1986. *Going International: How to Make Friends and Deal Effectively in the Global Marketplace.* New York: Plume.

Daft, R.L., and A.Y. Lewin. 1993. Where Are the Theories for the New Organization Forms? An Editorial Essay. *Organization Science* 4: i–vi.

de Bono, Edward. 1985. *Six Thinking Hats: An Essential Approach to Business Management.* Boston: Little, Brown.

Eisenberger, Naomi. 2009. Findings Presented at NeuroLeadership Summit. Available at www.neuroleadership.org/summits/2009-neuro leadership-summit.shtml.

Ekelund, B. Z., and E. Langvik. 2008. *Diversity Icebreaker: How to Manage Diversity Processes*. Oslo: Human Factors.

Friedman, Thomas. 2007. *The World Is Flat: A Brief History of the Twenty-First Century*. New York: Macmillan.

Giridharadas, Anand. 2010. New Leaders Find Strength in Diversity. *New York Times*, May 6.

Gordon, Evian. 2009. The Brain and Its Potential. YouTube video, www .youtube.com/v/d3rFNCPSfCU?fs=1&hl=en_US.

Hall, Edward T. 1976. *Beyond Culture*. Garden City, NY: Doubleday.

Hampden-Turner, Charles, and Fons Trompenaars. 2004. *Managing People across Cultures*. Chichester: Capstone.

Harris, Philip R., and Robert T. Moran. 1996. *Managing Cultural Differences: Leadership Strategies for a New World of Business*. 4th edition. Houston, TX: Gulf Professional Publishing.

Hart, Allen J., Paul J. Whalen, Lisa M. Shin, Sean C. McInerney, Håkan Fischer, and Scott L. Rauch. 2000. Differential Response in the Human Amygdala to Racial Outgroup vs. Ingroup Face Stimuli. *NeuroReport* 11: 2351–55.

Horstman, Judith. 2009. *The Scientific American Day in the Life of Your Brain: A 24-Hour Journal of What's Happening in Your Brain as You Sleep, Dream, Wake Up, Eat, Work, Play, Fight, Love, Worry, Compete, Hope, Make Important Decisions, Age and Change*. New York: John Wiley & Sons.

Iacoboni, Marco. 2008. *Mirroring People: The New Science of How We Connect with Others*. New York: Farrar, Straus & Giroux.

Isaacs, William. 1999. *Dialogue and the Art of Thinking Together: A Pioneering Approach to Communicating in Business and in Life*. New York: Random House.

Jia, L., E.R. Hirt, and S.C. Karpen. 2009. Lessons from a Faraway Land: The Effect of Spatial Distance on Creative Cognition. *Journal of Experimental Social Psychology* 45: 1127–31.

Just, Marcel Adam, and Sashank Varma. 2007. The Organization of Thinking: What Functional Brain Imaging Reveals about the

Neuroarchitecture of Complex Cognition. *Cognitive, Affective & Behavioral Neuroscience* 7: 153–91.

Lehrer, Jonah. 2007. *Proust was a Neuroscientist.* Boston: Houghton Mifflin Harcourt.

Lehrer, Jonah. 2009. Presentation at the NeuroLeadership Summit. Los Angeles, October 2009.

Mitchell, J.P., C.N. Macrae, and M.R. Banaji. 2006. Dissociable Medial Prefrontal Contributions to Judgments of Similar and Dissimilar Others. *Neuron* 50: 655–63.

Morrison, Terri, and Wayne A. Conaway. 2006. *Kiss, Bow or Shake Hands: The Bestselling Guide to Doing Business in More Than 60 Countries.* Cincinnati: Adams Media. Available at www.getcustoms.com or www.kissboworshakehands.com.

Ochsner, Kevin. 2008. Staying Cool under Pressure: Insights from Social Cognitive Neuroscience and Their Implications for Self and Society. *NeuroLeadership Journal* 1: 26–32.

Ochsner, K.N., and M.D. Lieberman. 2001. The Emergence of Social Cognitive Neuroscience. *American Psychologist* 56: 717–34.

Pearson, Christine, and Christine Porath. 2009. *The Cost of Bad Behavior: How Incivility Is Damaging Your Business and What to Do About It.* New York: Portfolio.

Rizzolatti, Giacomo, and Michael A. Arbib. 1998. Language within Our Grasp. *Trends in Neurosciences* 21: 188–94.

Rock, David. 2008. SCARF: A Brain-Based Model for Collaborating with and Influencing Others. *NeuroLeadership Journal* 1, no. 1 (December): 1–9.

Rosen, Christine. 2008. The Myth of Multitasking. *New Atlantis: A Journal of Technology & Society* 20: 105–10. Available at www.thenewatlantis.com/publications/the-myth-of-multitasking.

Rosinski, Philippe. 2003. *Coaching across Cultures: New Tools for Leveraging National, Corporate and Professional Differences.* Boston: Nicholas Brealey.

Ryan, Rosemary. 2003. Starbucks Launches Foray on France. September 26. www.bandt.com.au/news/starbucks-launches-foray-on-france.

Science Daily. 2007. Culture Is Key to Interpreting Facial Emotions. April 5.

Senge, Peter M., Art Kleiner, and Charlotte Roberts, eds. 1994. *The Fifth Discipline Fieldbook: Strategies and Tools for Building a Learning Organization.* New York: Currency Doubleday.

Siegel, Daniel. 2009. Findings Presented at NeuroLeadership Summit. Available at www.neuroleadership.org/summits/2009-neuro leadership-summit.shtml.

Subramanian, Ajay, Anand Venkateswaran, and Richard Fu. 2010. *Project Characteristics, Organizational Structure, and Managerial Incentives.* Social Science Research Network Paper. http://ssrn.com /abstract=1359799.

Timmons, Heather. 2010. Outsourcing to India Draws Western Lawyers. *New York Times*, August 4. www.nytimes.com/2010/08/05/business/global/05legal.html?scp=1&sq=lawyers%20outsource%20 to%20india&st=cse.

Toffler, Alvin. 1970. *Future Shock.* New York: Random House.

Tuckman, Bruce. 1965. Developmental Sequence in Small Groups. *Psychological Bulletin* 63, no. 6: 384–99. Available at www.mph.ufl.edu /events/seminar/Tuckman1965DevelopmentalSequence.pdf.

Tuckman, Bruce, and Mary Ann C. Jensen. 1977. Stages of Small Group Development Revisited. *Group and Organizational Studies* 2: 419-427.

Wall Street Journal. 1998. Work Week. CCXXII(126): A1. December.

Wiesenfeld, Batia M., Sumita Raghuram, and Raghu Garud. 1998. Communication Patterns as Determinants of Organizational Identification in a Virtual Organization. *Journal of Computer-Mediated Communication* 3, no 4. Available at http://jcmc.indiana.edu/vol3 /issue4/wiesenfeld.html.

Winters, Bradford D., Julius Pham, and Peter J. Pronovost. 2006. Rapid Response Teams: Walk, Don't Run. *Journal of the American Medical Association* 296: 1645–47.

About the Author

Maureen Bridget Rabotin, née Morley, founded Effective Global Leadership in 1996 to share her experience and knowledge with top executives, enabling them to leverage cross-cultural diversity for success. For more than a decade, she has designed and facilitated training programs for corporate clients involved in cross-cultural management, international negotiations, and global team building. Her practical experiences, passion for emotional and cultural intelligence, and interest in neuroscience have inspired this book and enabled her to coach and facilitate workshops for clients as they navigate the currents of globalization. She has worked for companies in a wide a range of industries, including luxury goods, finance, health care, and pharmaceuticals.

Rabotin is an executive coach certified by the International Coach Federation; she graduated from Northeastern University in Boston and studied at Advantara Institute in the United Kingdom, Mozaik International in France, and the Institute of Intercultural Communication, both in Oregon and Switzerland. Before founding Effective Global Leadership, she held management positions in a United States–based multinational as European product leader of microradiology and in a French electronics company as an export director. She has traveled and worked extensively throughout Europe, the Middle East, and Asia. She is married to a Frenchman and is the mother of two, and currently operates out of France and the United States. If you would like to learn more about Effective Global Leadership, visit www.effectivegloballeadership.com or contact the author at mrabotin@egleadership.com.

Index

Note: *f* represents a figure and *w* represents a worksheet.